Acknowledgements

I want to thank a few people who helped make this book possible. I would first like to thank God, my creator, and Jesus, my savior. Please believe those are not just words. I prayed almost daily before writing this book, asking for guidance and the ability to put on paper an accurate description of the recruiting system I was lucky enough to discover over the last 15 years. After you read this book, I'm sure you will agree that my prayers were answered. I would then like to thank the true entrepreneur who is holding this book right now. You might not realize it, but you are helping to keep the American Dream alive. Most people in America have forgotten that this country was built on *independence* not *dependence,* and the entrepreneurial spirit is what makes America great.

The next person I would like to thank is my wife Karen, who showed patience during the long hours and long weekends it took to write this book. I would also like to thank the master editor behind this book, Erin Fujimoto. Her expertise truly made this book possible. I could not have done it without her. I would also like to thank Herman Cortes the graphic artist that designed the cover. I can not forget my first and most important mentor in my networking career, Donny F. When I look back over our 15 years of friendship, I can honestly say that, although he was a man of little words, he taught me so much. Last, but certainly not least, I would like to thank my parents, Mike and Mary Demetro. They taught me that this world can be tough and you need to learn to stand on your own two feet, and never forget that money can bring you comfort, but only Jesus can bring you peace of mind. Out of everything I have learned on this journey we call life, I can honestly say those lessons by far have proven most valuable time and time again.

Sincerely

Mike Demetro

DO NOT SKIP OVER THE NEXT PAGE.

THE "INSIDER TELLS ALL" SYSTEM STARTS RIGHT NOW!!!

Top Secret Recruiting Breakthrough Just Revealed! This is your chance to be in front of a recruiting trend and NOT behind it!

WARNING: Only people who have actually ordered the newly released "Insider Tells All" book have been notified that the website below is LIVE! Here's why that's important to YOU!...

99.8% of ALL Networkers will never Discover this Website which gives you an incredible advantage over your competition!

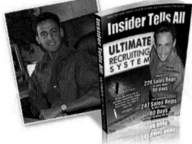

Dear Networker,

As the author of the "Insider Tells All" book, I would like to personally thank you for ordering the book and share some **EXTREMELY** time-sensitive information with you.

I feel this information is so important that I wanted to share it with you even before you had a chance to read this book. I am offering an extremely rare opportunity for you to receive a **FREE** gift valued at **$249.00** that has the real potential to **EXPLODE** your current down-line.

Now, I know this sounds like hype but trust me its only because you are an outsider looking in but that's all about to change. This is something so big you would never guess you could be a part of it. Please take a minute **RIGHT NOW** to visit the website shown below, it just went live and will explain everything!

www.InsidersMLMSecrets.com

P.S. This website will reveal one of network marketing's best kept recruiting secrets ever

Table of Contents

"If I Only Knew!"
What you don't know could be costing you a six-figure a year income.

What Is Network Marketing?
You will be shocked, angered, and most importantly, educated.

Picking the Right Company
Don't let the company pick you. Pick the company that's best for you.

What Is A Lead?
98% of network marketers do not know what a lead is. Do you?

Scripts
Knowing what not to say could be as important
as knowing what to say.

Generating Leads
Stop looking for a Big Hitter and become one.

Writing a Winning Ad
Bottom line: Writing a winning ad could make you rich.

Get your FREE website now
You can have your own website online in 15 minutes.

What can Google do for you
Millions of people are searching for a home business on Google.

"If I Only Knew!"

What you don't know could be costing you a six-figure a year income.

Insider Tells All Notes

* 2 Things are Required to Have a Profitable NWM Biz:

#1.) Sign up new people, &

#2.) Teach them to do the same.

Have you ever made the comment, "If only I knew!"? By the time you finish this short book from cover-to-cover, YOU WILL KNOW! This is not the "Think like a winner, and you will be a winner!" or "Just feel successful and you will magically be successful!" motivational mumbo-jumbo you might be accustomed to receiving (after you've paid, of course!)

This is REAL, no-holds-barred, solid information that provides you with a proven, step-by-step system to help ensure your success with any network marketing company. The SYSTEM you are about to discover is designed to help you:

S-ave Y-our S-elf T-ime E-nergy and M-oney

By the time you finish this book there will be no questions unanswered and no stones left unturned. You will know exactly what to do and even what to say to build your new or existing business.

VERY IMPORTANT: Do not skip ahead in this book, it will only confuse you. Each chapter contains an important piece to a marketing puzzle that cannot be overlooked or passed over. Trust me on this. This book does not contain a story. It contains an actual marketing system on which your business will run. If you take the time to read this book in the order it was written, chapter by chapter, you will discover a simple and powerful marketing system for your network marketing business to be built upon.

Entrepreneur Magazine says that 97% of people who start a home business will fail if they do not have a marketing system in place.

The good news is that 94% of people who start a home business with a proven marketing system in place to help ensure their success go on to create a substantial income! A certain amount of them will actually go on to become MILLIONAIRES!

DO NOT put off reading this book one more day. Every moment you wait could cost you hundreds, even thousands, of dollars!
Turn off the television and give this book and your network marketing business the attention they deserve.

You should be able to read this entire book from cover to cover in as little as 3 hours.

This book could have easily been 300 or 400 pages long and filled with a bunch of fluff like many of the "How To" programs and books I have seen, but that's not what I had in mind when it was written.

I wanted to write a book that would be simple, easy to understand, and easy to follow. A book that gets right to the point and gives you, the entrepreneur, a real system that you can use to immediately jump-start any network marketing business!

You are now just 3 short hours away from discovering a system that has allowed me to personally sponsor over 247 people in less than 80 days! And I have done this three times with three different companies!

What exactly does this mean to you? It means...

Three totally different network marketing companies, one simple system, same incredible results!

Think about what I just said! What would 20 or even 40 new recruits mean to your network marketing business, not to mention your check? That's the very reason I'm asking you to find 3 hours out of the next 48 to read this book cover to cover.

Before we get started, I feel that I need to tell you a little bit about myself and where I have been in the industry of network marketing so you can get an idea of where we can go together.

When I was 3, I got my first bicycle. It was red. I loved that bicycle. I rode that bike everywhere. Okay, I'm just kidding! I wouldn't do that to you. But seriously, at the age of 23 I started my first business. It was a vending company in Houston, Texas. You know... soda machines! By the time I was 24, I had 72 machines all over Houston. I was making great money for a 24-year old. I owned a BMW that I purchased with cash and had a cell phone that was as big and heavy as a brick. Keep in mind the year was 1995. Bottom-line, I was successful and my own boss. Here was the problem.

My life consisted of filling those machines from sun up to sun down, six days a week. One morning at 5 a.m., I was sitting in my cargo van in the rain, with the flu, waiting for my daily delivery of 150 cases of soda that I would have to load by myself.

It took three hours for my van to be loaded, and I was now ready to start my work day and fill at least 50 machines. It was at that moment I knew there had to be an easier and better way to get my piece of the 'American Dream'.

Within six months, I sold that company, including the van, and decided to start another business - one with less manual labor and more income. After doing research for almost 90 days, I decided network marketing was the way to go simply because network marketing is the best chance for the average person, like you and me, to create a multimillion dollar distributorship with no employees and a minimal investment!

I jumped in with both feet and hit the ground running. Selling my previous business gave me enough money to dedicate 40 to 50 hours a week to my network marketing career. Fast forward two years later, and I was now almost out of money. On top of that, I wasn't any closer to creating a stable or even profitable income than the day I started.

I tried it all: home meetings, company meetings, flyers, radio, even television. This is where you will realize that no matter how long you have been in the network marketing industry or what you have been through, I can honestly say, "I have been there, done that, and bought the t-shirt!"

Within those 2 years I joined at least 3 different companies, and no matter how hard I tried I couldn't turn a profit. I even took one of the network marketing company's 30-minute videotapes and made 500 copies (which wasn't cheap!) I then walked my entire subdivision hanging a tape on each door with a simple letter asking people to watch my 30-minute videotape about creating wealth from home. I also asked them to simply put it back on the door the next morning if they were not interested. Within 48 hours, I had successfully lost all of my videotapes, and I am embarrassed to say, did not sign up one new person in my business.

I felt like I needed to tell you this short story to confirm in your mind that, no matter what you have been through in network marketing, I have been there. However, there is a happy ending to this story. Now that you have my book in your hands, I truly believe there will be a happy ending for you as well.

So let me finish my story...

It was now 2 years since the day I started my network marketing career, and my videotape plan did not work. I had the time and money for one last attempt at building a successful home business before it was time to start looking for a job.

With the last of my savings, I decided to shoot a 30-second television commercial about building wealth from home. After the production of the commercial and air time was paid for, I was officially out of time and broke.

The commercial was almost at the end of its 15 day run on TV, and from all accounts appeared to be yet another failure. Then, out of the blue, it happened! The phone rang! The person at the other end of the phone was up late the night before and happened to see my commercial. He told me that he liked what he saw and wanted to meet me at his home.

I thought, "Great! This will be a new distributor in my business, and it may be just enough to keep my network marketing dream alive."

When I pulled up to this gentleman's home, it was more like an estate, complete with a red Ferrari and black Mercedes parked out front.

This home came complete with a two story night club and not 1 or 2 but 3 separate pools to swim in. It also had a movie theater and I'm not talking about a home theater system. This estate had a full size movie theater complete with a snack bar and ticket booth. Now I'm not telling you all this to impress you but rather to impress

14

upon you what is possible when you have a proven marketing system combined with the power of direct marketing or Multi level marketing. OK, back to my story…

Pictures of the actual home

This home was in an area of Houston, Texas that can best be compared to Beverly Hills. I immediately thought, "Wow, I just hit the Mother Lode! This guy will join my business and spend thousands of dollars running my television commercial on every major channel!"

Nothing could have been further from the truth. Within minutes of talking with him, I immediately knew that he was not about to join my business. In fact, I was about to join his network marketing company, a company he <u>owned</u>!

The following Monday I went to his office, which was really a professional telemarketing room with over 100 employees. The very moment the elevator doors opened on the 8th floor I immediately knew what I had been doing wrong all these years.

The simple system I discovered that day, and in the months and years that followed, allowed me to recruit up to 14 new people in a single day. What makes this even more impressive is the fact that the new people joining my network marketing business were total strangers!

I went from being one of those guys at the network marketing meeting embarrassed to tell you how many people I had in my downline to being the guy on the stage explaining to people how I'm having so much success in such a short amount of time!

The same incredible systems and techniques that you are about to

15

discover in this book have allowed me to be featured on a television show about building wealth from home viewed by millions.

The systems, techniques and flat out marketing strategies I have learned over the last 15 years are all contained within this book, but that's not all. This book also contains the information needed to solve two of network marketing's biggest problems.

The FIRST major problem in network marketing is what I refer to as the **"Blind-Leading-the-Blind"**.

Let me explain, let's say your friend or family member introduces you to a network marketing company and you decide to join because you like the product and idea of owning a home business.

HOWEVER, chances are your friend or family member has not figured out herself how to make money and recruit new people. So ask yourself, "How is she supposed to tell you how to make money and recruit new people?" Exactly! That's why I call it the **"Blind-Leading-the-Blind"**!

The second problem is that most people DO NOT want to talk to friends and family when trying to build their business. This is usually a hard sell for the simple fact that, as soon as they ask you the million dollar question, "How much money have you made?", it's 'Game Over'!

Those are the two major problems with network marketing. The good news is this book will solve both problems!

So...let's get started right now!

If you have been in network marketing for any time at all, you should have figured out that you basically have two jobs.

FIRST, to sign-up new customers and distributors in your business and…

SECOND, train them to do the same!

It's that simple.

By the time you finish this short book you will know how to find total strangers and put them in the business. The only thing left to do is train them to do the same. You won't believe how simple this is going to be. Take a minute **RIGHT NOW** to e-mail or call every person in your current network marketing business and give them the following website address.

www.InsiderTellsAll.com

Now they can get a copy of this book and get the same cutting-edge training as you are right now! This is so everyone in your business will be on the same page at the same time.

Having just 5 or 10 people in your downline, trained to make massive exposures (which this book teaches), is the very thing capable of delivering an income of $20,000 or $30,000 per month!

What I want you to understand is that the only difference between you and me is that I have already been down that long, long road of mistakes that every person, no matter how smart they are, will make.

This is called a "learning curve". The faster you get through the learning curve, the better. That is what this book is meant to do - get you through that curve, and on to profits as soon as possible.

If you are serious about being successful in this industry you need to be teachable and coachable. For example, at this point in the book we have already taken the first step in getting your network marketing business off the ground.

Take a minute right now *(NOT LATER)* to e-mail or call every person in your downline to let them know that they need to go to www.InsiderTellsAll.com to get a copy of this book today.

Remember, two things are required to have a profitable network marketing business: sign up new people, and train them to do the same.

By the time you finish this book, you will know how to sign up total strangers in your business, and by getting this book in the hands of your downline today, you will train them to do the same.

What Is Network Marketing?

You will be shocked, angered, and most importantly, educated.

Insider Tells All Notes

Network marketing has been around now for almost 70 years, and shows no signs of slowing down. In fact, if anything, it is now gaining more popularity due to the power of the internet. Simply put, network marketing or multi-level marketing is absolutely the best chance for the average person to create an above average income, and in some cases, a multi-million dollar distributorship right from the comfort of his own home.

The absolute benefit to network marketing is the low start-up costs. A person can actually start a home business equipped with a website for as little as one-hundred dollars! Another benefit to keep in mind is that the network marketing company, in most cases, will maintain your website and handle product development and shipping. It will also handle all your accounting needs, book keeping, payroll, and training of new distributors.

Thus, you can see network marketing is without a doubt the best chance for the average person to create a multi-million dollar distributorship that is nationwide, and in some cases, worldwide, right from his own home. Sit back and put your feet up because you are about to be shocked, possibly angered, but most importantly, informed and educated about network marketing!

At this point, let's review. I want to go over the positives in network marketing before I cover the negatives. Remember, a good network marketing company handles website maintenance and development, product development and shipping, bookkeeping and payroll, and most importantly, training.

Now, let's talk about the negatives and what you need to stay clear of. You will notice the word "network marketing" has the word "marketing" in it. The power of two people turning into ten people who turn into a thousand people is the essence of network marketing and can be referred to as "Grass Roots", or more recently, "Viral Marketing". No matter what you call it, this is still one of the strongest forms of marketing there is.

Let me give you a few examples of how powerful network marketing truly is. Did you know back in the 1990's when long distance calling was deregulated, which simply means that other companies were allowed to solicit your business, the first two companies that stepped up to tackle this challenge and get people to switch from AT&T were two small and unheard of companies called Sprint and MCI? These two companies tried direct mail, television, and even radio. They also had telemarketing rooms that would call people directly and try to get them to switch their long distance from AT&T to Sprint or MCI.

Believe it or not, no matter what they did, they could not convince the average person to switch, even though their rates were less than AT&T's! People were just not ready to take a chance on an unknown startup company with their long distance phone service. In Sprint and MCI's last attempt to break into the long distance market and get their fair share, they decided to use the power of network marketing.

MCI decided to go with Amway, a network marketing company that every person in America has heard of, to distribute their long distance service. Sprint allowed a network marketing company called Network 2000 to distribute their long distance service. Network 2000 brought this new and unheard of company called Sprint one million customers in 9 short months, something that even television and radio could not accomplish! Welcome to the wonderful world of network marketing!

Long story short, Sprint and MCI are now household names, and they owe it all to the power of network marketing. Just a few more examples before we move on. Did you know that vitamins are a multi-billion dollar industry? To this day, Amway is still one of the largest, if not THE largest, distributor of vitamins around the world.

Cosmetics are also a multi-billion dollar industry. To this day, due to the power of network marketing, Avon and Mary Kay Cosmetics have claimed the largest market share of the cosmetic industry. Let me give you one last example of the power and versatility of network marketing. When you think of that leftover meatloaf sitting in the Tupperware container, did you know that chances are, Tupperware found its way into your home via the power of network marketing? Now I hope you understand how big this really is.

The downside and first negative is that some network marketing companies have realized that network marketing is such a strong vehicle for distribution that they are able to attach a bogus or hokey product or service to a network marketing company and still generate millions of dollars in sales. You, as an independent business owner, need to ask yourself one simple question when evaluating a network marketing company. "Can this product or service stand alone and be sold in stores if it didn't have the power of network marketing to distribute it?"

A strong product line or service is the very thing that will allow you to eventually walk away from your distributorship and continue to receive checks for years to come. This is called residual income.

The second negative in network marketing, is the term I mentioned earlier: the "Blind-Leading-the-Blind". I feel is the biggest problem in network marketing and the very reason I wrote this book. You will read throughout this book that TRAINING is the key to your success. As you read this book, you are being trained. To ensure the success of your downline, as well as your own, your recruits need to be trained as well!

If you have one, ten, or even a hundred people in your downline, this is the best advice I can give you. With that being said, let me ask you a question to see how serious you truly are about having a successful network marketing career. Are you ready for the question?

Did you e-mail or call your downline to let them know where to get a copy of this book?

If you answered, "YES", that's great! It means you are teachable and are off to a good start. If you have not emailed or called every person in your downline and given them the **www.InsiderTellsAll.com** address, you need to do so right now.

I'm serious! It is not doing anyone any good for people to spend $200 or $300 to sign up as distributors in your downline if you are not giving them the training they need to be successful. A few chapters from now you will see and understand why this is so very important. Let me give you an example of why training your team or downline is one of the most important things you can do when trying to build your check to $10,000 a month.

When a network marketing company gains momentum, it can easily go from 1,000 distributors to as many as 10,000 distributors in a 60-day period.

The problem with growth like this is that some people can be misled with common phrases such as "just get in at the beginning" and "you don't have to do anything and you will get rich" or the ever-popular "just get two people and you will make a million dollars because this is the right deal at the right time".

These are the very statements that mislead people and put a bad taste in their mouth. It tarnishes the powerful and wonderful world of network marketing.

Think about it, if it were as easy as joining a company for two or three hundred dollars and the momentum of the company itself will make you a millionaire with no work, why wouldn't the owner of the network marketing company simply keep the bulk of his company for himself and keep all the profits that are about to roll in from this magic momentum?

Why would he let total strangers buy into his company for pennies on the dollar and become millionaires with little to no work on their behalf? Exactly. It sounds stupid when I put it like that. Starting a network marketing distributorship is NOT like buying stock!

You don't just get in and get rich without working! Building a successful network marketing distributorship starts with a simple product or service that makes sense and will sell for a fair price.

Even though the network marketing company will take care of your website, product, and bookkeeping, it is your job to expose your product or service to the market and create sales just as it would be for a traditional business.

Think about this. How ridiculous does it sound to be involved with a company or business, and all you have to do to become a millionaire is generate two or three sales? It's amazing what some people will believe when the 'greed factor' kicks in.

The truth is you have one important job when starting your new network marketing distributorship, and that is to **expose** your product or service to as many people as you can as fast as you can! The good news is that by the end of this short book I will have given you simple, step-by-step instructions on how to expose your product or service to thousands of people every single day without ever leaving your home!

Once again, what I am about to say needs to be repeated because it is that important. In real estate, you have heard the term "location, location, location"? In network marketing, you should now realize that it is called

"EXPOSURES, EXPOSURES, EXPOSURES!"

As good as the pitch sounds, *"You're in at the beginning"*, I would like to tell you that it doesn't mean **ANYTHING!** Your success all comes down to the amount of exposures you make on a daily basis. It's really simple. The three faces shown below represent the three major personalities and people you will run across in sales. It doesn't matter if you're selling helicopter blades, dump trucks, or a network marketing opportunity. When I say you need to make as many exposures as possible, I say that because your goal is to find as many happy faces as soon as possible.

Let me explain.

The first face shown with the smile represents a person that is opened minded and optimistic. This is someone who would probably join your business with little to no effort on your behalf.

The second face with the straight line for the mouth is someone that I would refer to as an engineer type. This person will take a little longer to put in your network marketing business. He is analytical and will ask a lot of questions before making a decision.

The third face with the frown is someone that will never join your business. This type of person gets up every day at 5:00 a.m. to go to a job he hates where he works for a boss he doesn't like, but will never do anything to change his circumstances! You could pull a rock out of their flower bed, and sprinkle your magic MLM dust on it, and turn that rock into solid gold, and he still wouldn't join your business! What do you do when you run across a person like this? Simple: **NEXT!!!**

You should see by this simple example that you're not selling, you're really sorting. You simply need to find as many smiley faces as fast as you can! Accordingly, that's why leads, scripts, and this **BOOK** are worth their weight in **GOLD**! The top money earners in network marketing companies are simply the people who make the most exposures on a daily basis.

Understanding network marketing and getting educated just as you are right now is a great investment in your financial future. What you are doing right now is shortening the learning curve that comes with every business and, at the same time, discovering a proven marketing system on which your business can run.

Imagine being able to join a network marketing company and put 30 new people in your business personally in 30 days. That is what is possible when you understand your goal, and have a proven marketing system to accomplish that goal. With that being said, I want to clear up another urban legend before we go any further.

If you are looking for some mythical, do nothing, say nothing, auto-recruiting system that magically allows a person to push a few buttons on her computer each day for a few minutes and watch her downline explode, you won't find it. This book does not contain any such system for the simple fact that a magical auto-recruiting system like that DOES NOT EXIST!

Think about it…if there were such a system, wouldn't the multi- million dollar network marketing companies out there use it for themselves to sell their own products and services and do away with all their distributors? They would save themselves millions of dollars in commissions each year.

I still communicate with a handful of the top network marketers from around the country and we all agree that no such auto-recruiting system exists.

I will say that there are tricks and strategies for collecting and generating leads that will make your downline grow like magic when they are used in conjunction with a good script and auto-training system. The good news is that all of the strategies, techniques and auto-training I just talked about are all contained in this book.

This book contains a 100% real system that works if you are willing to follow the simple instructions. The system in this book revolves around leads, scripts, and auto-training. Once you have learned and apply the systems within this book you will become very valuable to the network marketing industry; an industry which is coming into its own. Your timing is perfect.

Network marketing has been around for almost 70 years with absolutely no signs of slowing down. In fact, it is just beginning to enter mainstream America like never before. We all know someone who is currently in a network marketing company or has joined one in the past.

You may have even seen commercials recently on major television networks for Avon and Amway. Even while writing this book I watched a prime time television show that featured a product from a network marketing company. Here is what all of this means to you.

When radio was invented, the major players who became rich were taking part in an unknown communication and advertising vehicle that was not taught in high school or college! They were pioneers who had to find their education by any means necessary. The same holds true for television. When television replaced radio as the number one communication and advertising vehicle, the major players who got rich and became multi-millionaires were pioneers.

Basically, what I am telling you right now is that you are truly a pioneer! You cannot take network marketing classes in high school or college. You are on the absolute forefront of an industry ready to come into its own.

Here is the great news. When you learn the simple but effective systems in this book and learn how to utilize the internet and technology to expose your product or service to the masses, you will become a leader in this industry. As a result, you will be sought after by individual people and even other companies!

Within months, not years, of discovering the marketing tips and systems in this book, I was featured on television. I also had my name appear in countless home business magazines and had network marketing companies give me complimentary spots within their companies. This ended up generating thousands and thousands of dollars for me with absolutely no work on my behalf more than a few times!

I've even had a company offer to send a private plane to pick me up to tour their home office! All of this was simply because I learned how to expose a networking marketing product or service to the masses right from the comfort of home.

So, my hope for you is that through reading this book **RIGHT NOW**, you will learn in just a few short hours what took me years of hard work, thousands of dollars, a strong desire, and to be quite honest, a little luck, to uncover!

Picking the Right Company

Don't let the company pick you. Pick the company that's best for you.

Insider Tells All Notes

Choosing the right company in network marketing is one of the biggest decisions that you are going to make. Think about it. You are going to pick not just a company, but literally a business partner!

The company will expect you to expose its product and business opportunity to the masses. Likewise, you will expect several things from the company that I think we need to cover right now. It is the network marketing company's responsibility to host and maintain each distributor's website along with bookkeeping and payroll.

If you were to build a distributorship of thousands of people that stretches nationwide and in some cases into other countries, the network marketing company would have to keep track of that entire product being distributed. In addition, it would have to stay on top of payroll for the thousand or more people in your new organization.

The network marketing company will also need to take care of product development and shipping. Keep in mind, your job is simply to expose the company's product and business opportunity to as many people as you can!

When you look at it like this, it seems as though the distributor has a lot less responsibility and gets the better deal! I personally know of more than a handful of network marketing millionaires who have had plenty of opportunities to start or be involved with the ownership of a company and wanted no part of it! I myself have been a consultant and worked behind the scenes for a few different companies to help get them off the ground, and can tell you personally that I want no part of the corporate end of network marketing! I am perfectly happy being a distributor.

With that being said, I don't want to give you the wrong idea. When you start your own network marketing distributorship, you own that distributorship. It is literally a small company that you own and are building within a bigger company! If you want to sell it as an outright business or even pass it on to a family member that is well within your right. The most important thing a network marketing company should provide for its distributors is access to the best marketing materials possible.

The marketing materials that you will use to build your distributorship are almost as important as the product itself. When evaluating a network marketing company's marketing materials, make sure it is utilizing today's technology to the fullest! In this age and time, what you are really looking for is a turnkey internet marketing system.

Let me give you an example. I can't think of any network marketing company at this time that does not supply its distributors with a self-replicating website. This simply means that you would have your own personal website linked directly to you that is an exact replica of the company's website, except in certain areas it will have your contact information and distributor number instead of the company's.

Now let's get back to marketing materials. An example of good marketing materials and a turnkey marketing system would be a website containing a simple video explaining the product and business opportunity which can be viewed by anyone nationwide who has a computer. This will allow you to show people a mini-internet infomercial that does 60% of the work for you with the simple click of a button. Another example of a turnkey marketing system is yet another video, or in some cases, an audio that will also explain the compensation or pay plan as it is commonly known.

Let's imagine the turnkey internet marketing system that I just described in action. A new distributor who joins your business can now send new prospects to his website. With a simple click of a button, he can show that new prospect two or three videos explaining the product, the business opportunity, and how to get paid without having to say a word! At this point you should have a good idea of what you are looking for in the form of marketing materials that should be provided by the network marketing company.

In some cases, network marketing companies are even able to get their product or service on the cover of well known magazines and major news networks. They have also had celebrities endorse their products or services. This provides credibility, and can never hurt! When this type of credibility is put into a video format and played right from your personal website, you will find that it makes your job as a distributor a lot easier.

The last thing I would like to say about choosing a company before we move on to product is you really have to decide if you want to go with an established company that has been around for a few decades versus a start-up company. Each one definitely has its own "pros and cons". When going with an established company with a household name, you obviously have a strong product line and stability. It has stood the test of time and has a loyal customer base.

The problem you can run into is that when exposing the product and business opportunity to the masses, it is a little harder to create excitement with a business opportunity that most people have already heard of. Fundamentally, you are not bringing them the newest and greatest business that is about to sweep the nation.

Your strongpoint when marketing a company with a household name is obviously stability, and the fact that they have hundreds or even thousands of people making a substantial income. When choosing to work with a start-up or new company that has only been around for a year or two, you now have, in most cases, the excitement of a product or service that has never been available before. You also have a new business opportunity that nobody has ever heard of. As a result, this situation presents the opportunity to be a part of something great by being involved with an exciting new business.
The obvious negative here is without a proven track record or longevity, you are trading stability for the opportunity to work with a product that the masses have not been introduced to yet.

When choosing a company, keep in mind that you are also choosing a product. A product is actually the foundation of your business opportunity. If you have spent any time in the network marketing industry you have most likely realized that there are a variety of products and services to choose from! For instance, there is travel, healthcare products, cosmetics, software-related products, and even legal services. The list goes on and on.

When choosing a product, the first thing you must do is find a product you are passionate about. If health and nutrition is your passion then you would obviously lean towards a health and nutrition network marketing company.

The second thing that you need to do after choosing a product is to become a product of that product. Here's what I mean by that. Use that product immediately. If you were to choose a weight loss product, you should use that product to see how much weight you will actually lose. If you decide to market cosmetics, use those cosmetics immediately to see how they compare to other cosmetics in the marketplace. Becoming a product of the product is going to accomplish two very important things. Number one is obviously product knowledge that you will gain by simply using the product. Number two, your belief in the product will increase when you experience results from that product.

For example, if it is a weight loss product and you lose weight, your belief in that product will obviously increase. If you are marketing, let's say a discount travel package, and you go on a discount vacation and have a great time, once again, your belief factor will increase.

This is a very important step in launching your business for two very important reasons. When you present your product and business opportunity, it's not just what you say, **but how you say it.** When you present your business opportunity and product to a person who is skeptical or negative, you will be able to debate with that person from a position of strength because you know the product or service delivers on its promise. Why? Because you have experienced the results firsthand.

The last thing we need to cover in this chapter is sponsorship. We have already talked about choosing the company that is right for you and making sure that they have an automated marketing and training system in place. We also covered what you need to consider when choosing the product that is best for you. The last thing we need to cover is sponsorship, and this is important.

When joining a network marketing company, you will most likely be joining under another distributor. This is a person who signed up and started his network marketing business just as you would. The major problem, and the very reason I'm writing this book is because this is where you are most likely to run into a case of the "blind leading the blind."

Recall when I mentioned earlier that signing up two or three people a week in your business (depending on your compensation plan) can generate a monthly income of about $1,000. Conversely, training those people to do the same is what could potentially deliver twenty, thirty, or even forty thousand dollars per month.

Now let's go back to the "blind leading the blind".

The person who is presenting you with this business opportunity could very well have the best intentions, but if she has never been able to generate an income of, let's say, four thousand dollars per month, how is he supposed to tell you how to create that kind of income? This is what I call the "blind leading the blind". When I am presented with a business opportunity in which I have decided the product is marketable, I then put the person sponsoring me through an interview process. Questions I will immediately ask are: "How many people do you currently have in your business, and how many people have you personally sponsored yourself?"

These two questions will give you a great snapshot of your sponsor's capabilities. For instance, if she personally sponsored twenty or more people, she obviously has a stable recruiting system in place for putting new people in her business. However, if she personally sponsored twenty people herself, but only had a total of twenty five people in her business, this would lead me to believe that she is lacking in the training and duplication department.

If a person has only sponsored two people personally, this would tell me that she does not have a decent recruiting system in place for putting new people in her business. However, if a person has only personally sponsored two people but has a team or distributorship of one hundred or more people, this would tell me that she has a good training system in place and is creating duplication within her business.

You may want to read over the above three paragraphs to truly understand what I'm telling you here. The example above is the best way for you to understand your sponsor's capabilities. The last thing you will want to evaluate when choosing your sponsor is exactly what her commitment level is to helping you get your business off the ground. You can discover this by asking a few simple questions.

The first question I would ask my potential sponsor is, "How many hours a day do you plan to spend on building this business?" This question alone will give you a good idea if she plans to do this business part time or full time.

The second question to ask is, "What training or support do you have in place outside of what the network marketing company offers?"

The last question you should ask is, "What marketing or recruiting systems do you have in place outside of what the company offers?"

These questions will give you a good overview of your potential sponsor's commitment to helping you get your business up and running. The last thing I would like to say in closing is when choosing your potential sponsor do not be afraid to go upline to get as much support as you possibly can.

Let me explain. On more than a few occasions in my career, I ended up joining under my sponsor whom we will call Joe. Shortly after launching my business, I realized Joe's commitment did not match my own. I was ready to work three hours a day and his commitment level was to work only three hours a week.

In this case, I went upline to the person who sponsored Joe. We'll call him Frank. Frank was prepared to commit three hours a day to help me build my business because he also benefits from the growth and volume that my distributorship produces.

The moral to the story is when choosing your sponsor ask as many questions as possible. Think of it as if you were interviewing them for a business partner.

Remember not to be afraid of going upline one, two, or even three people to get as much information as you can from each sponsor. Mainly, because you may need the support and training that they could offer outside of what the network marketing company offers.

What Is A Lead?

98% of network marketers do not know what a lead is. Do you?

Insider Tells All Notes

Before we get to the chapter, "Generating Leads", I knew this chapter, "What is a Lead?" needed to be written. I'll tell you why.

Leads can literally make or break your career in network marketing. In fact, even traditional companies that deal with sales depend on leads for their survival. The reason I knew I had to write this chapter was simple. I was on stage speaking in front of 300 people at a network marketing meeting. When I asked the audience by a show of hands, "How many people know what a lead is?" I was shocked when only twenty or thirty hands went up.

Actual Meeting

Out of 300 people, only 20 or 30 hands went up...

That's a
BIG problem

That is why this chapter needed to be written.

I struggled in network marketing for almost two years until I discovered what a lead is. The cold hard truth is that most people who join a network marketing company never have the opportunity to discover leads and how to use them effectively.

Unfortunately, most people join a network marketing company, talk to a few people, get rejected, and are out of business before they ever get a single check. This business is not a hobby. It is a true business. People in network marketing usually talk to their brother and cousin and get rejected, or in some cases, sign them up as a new distributor and then stop working.

Remember the two biggest problems with network marketing are people telling other people, "just buy a spot in the company - you won't have to do anything and you're going to get rich.", or my favorite, "just sign up two people and you're done."

Think about how crazy this sounds. Can you name any other business in the entire world that can make you rich with two sales? Imagine being a car salesman and showing up to work knowing that if you just sell two cars your job is done, and you will now become a millionaire. Do you get my point?

Network marketing is truly the best chance for the average person to become a millionaire by working from the comfort of his own home but network marketing is not magic. Building a network marketing distributorship is just like building an actual company.

If you have been in network marketing for any amount of time, then you know almost every company has people/distributors who are making thirty or forty thousand dollars a month. At the same time, other people in the same exact company selling the same exact products or services will not be able to receive one single check. Why is this?

It all comes down to one single word: **EXPOSURES!!!** It is that simple. The people you hear about who are making thirty and forty thousand dollars a month have simply learned how to expose their product and network marketing opportunity to the masses and train their downline to do the same. I have told you twice already in this book to e-mail or call your downline so you can give them the website address, **www.InsiderTellsAll.com**, so they can get a copy of this book and GET TRAINED!

If you have not done so by this point I have to say that is not a good sign when it comes to being teachable and coachable. Let's return to leads. Do you talk to your cousin, brother, and friend about your new business to see if they would like to join? Sure you do!

Nevertheless, you ALSO need to ask twenty other people that same day if they would like to join your business.

That is where leads come in, and that is what this book is all about: getting and creating leads, so you and your DOWNLINE will have new people every day you can expose your product and business opportunity to.

The key to working leads correctly is to stay organized and efficient, which brings up a good point. I can't tell you how many times I've gotten off stage after a network marketing training and had people surround me telling me that they want to make twenty thousand dollars a month. When I proceed to ask them if they have a simple business card, nine times out of ten, they don't have one!

The first thought in my head is this person wants to make twenty thousand dollars a month and enjoy the lifestyle and freedom that comes along with that kind of money, but she doesn't even have a business card? It sounds crazy, but it's true. I'll take it one step further. I can't tell you how many times I have given training seminars in which I am sharing marketing secrets that millionaires I have worked with use to pull in $50,000 in sales in a single day, and have looked out in the audience to see that some people don't even have a pen and paper to take notes.

Remember, network marketing is the best chance for a person to get rich with a $100 to $500 investment, but it is not magic!!! Think about this. If you were going to open a fast food franchise, I would guess that you would have to go to some special classes or even some type of "hamburger university" before you could even think about opening your franchise to sell something as simple as hamburgers.

On top of that, once your store opened, you would need to have multiple computers and countless notebooks and binders to help run your business. This being a business that I would guess would generate two hundred thousand dollars a year in income if you're lucky.

Hence, you can see how this would shock me when a network marketing distributorship could easily generate two to three hundred thousand dollars a year income, and you have people who believe they can do this without having business cards or even a single notebook dedicated to their company.

The good news is, since the network marketing company will take care of payroll, bookkeeping, website maintenance, product development, and shipping, I'm going to show you how it is possible to run your network marketing business from one single 3-ring binder.

When you are talking to 20 people a day, which I'm going to show you how to do in the next chapter, you are going to need to stay organized.

This is why I'm going to ask you for a second time not to skip ahead in this book like some people do. I will be helping you set up your 3-ring binder later in this chapter. Setting up our binder is a very important process when working with leads, and that is what this chapter will cover. Before we actually set up our binder, I want to take a minute to finish talking about what a lead actually is.

A lead is simply a name, number, and email address of a person who has shown an interest in your product, service, or business opportunity. There are many ways to find these people and we will get to that in a minute. First, we will talk about warm market leads. The beauty of network marketing is that, along with a product or service that a person might want to buy, you also offer them the opportunity to make money from home. A warm market lead is someone who needs to make extra money or is not happy with their current job or career.

A warm market lead could also be someone you think could benefit from the product or service your network marketing business offers and not necessarily the business opportunity. Don't forget, you are looking for customers as well as new people to join your business.

When making your warm market list (your leads), you need to come up with at least thirty to forty names and phone numbers. If you don't know thirty to forty people who could benefit from making extra money, keep trying. Remember, 98% of the U.S., your friends and family included, worry about money on a daily, if not hourly, basis (more on that in a minute).

Also keep in mind that most network marketing companies are nationwide, so you are not limited to people in your immediate area. There are several phone companies these days offering flat fee long distance programs, so there are NO long distance bills standing in your way when it comes to calling people all across the U.S.

Back in the day, a network marketing distributor, myself included, would have to budget in a four or five hundred dollar long distance bill each month. I'm happy to say that's a thing of the past, and network marketing played a big role in that. Now that we have covered warm market leads, I would like to take time to talk to you about lead brokers so you can see just one simple way to find total strangers to expose your business to.

Remember, when building your business, you need to talk to 20 people a day. I'm going to show one way that you can do that right now. Did you know that you can go to Google or Yahoo and simply search for any of the following and hundreds of lead brokers will come up?

home business leads
network marketing leads
business opportunity leads

Home Business Leads

Now, if you're saying to yourself, Mike, I have known about leads and lead brokers for a while now, well let me ask you a very important question. Does your entire downline know about them? Are you willing to bet your check on it because that's exactly what you're betting with, YOUR CHECK!

Remember, this is not just a book it's also an auto training system that will train your downline for you. This is why I instructed you to email your entire downline the Insider Tells All.com link so that they can get a copy & learn about leads & lead brokers in case they were unaware. Knowing about leads/lead brokers is too important to leave to chance.

I'm going to tell you right now that you have to be extremely careful when purchasing leads. Remember, you are just buying names, phone numbers, and in some cases, e-mail addresses from a stranger who is telling you that the people on your list have responded to some form of advertisement about creating an income from home. In every industry you have to be careful who you do business with, and lead brokers are no different.

It is very important when purchasing leads that you get the email addresses in addition to the names and phone numbers. You will see why this is so important later in the book when we talk about the "fortune is in the follow-up". A lead broker will usually break leads up into categories by time, which simply means the date the lead was created. The newer the lead, the better. Here's an example. The broker may try to sell you a list of names and phone numbers for $1.00 each because these people have supposedly responded to an internet form or mailer about making money from home in the last 48 hours.

If you don't want to pay $1.00 per name, he might offer to sell you a list of names and phone numbers for $.50 a person because these people supposedly responded to an internet form or mailer about making money in the past 30 days. The broker will probably tell you that you will get a much better response from the $1.00 leads because they are only 48 hours old. That is normally a true statement.

Here is the problem. Unfortunately, there is really no way to know how old the lead you are getting is, so 9 times out of 10 I will go with the $.50 leads. I will tell you the more questions you ask, the better. I also believe a good script (what you will say to these people) can make $.50 cent leads perform like $1 leads. Don't worry. We will also cover "**Scripts**" in the next few chapters. Here is something exciting to think about. You now understand a little more about lead brokers. Imagine having just 5 people in your downline who read this book and are planning to buy leads from a broker.

This is why I have said it is very important to get your downline to www.InsiderTellsAll.com as soon as possible to get a copy of this book. After the people in your downline have read this book and order leads like professional sales people, they all can now start to expose their businesses to 20 new people a day. That's why this book was written...massive duplication.

Let's take this one step further. If five distributors in your business each make 20 exposures a day, that's 100 calls a day being made to help build their business and YOURS. In one month, just a 5-man downline would make about 3,000 exposures.

Do you see why it is important to get this book in every person's hand in your current network marketing business as soon as possible? It will tell your downline how to find new people through leads and in a minute it will even tell them what to say, AND WE ARE JUST GETTING STARTED.

When working with leads, you will quickly discover that it is easier to talk to strangers than it is to friends and family about a business opportunity. This actually makes it easier for you and your downline to get your businesses up and running. Let's go back to the moral of this story. When it comes to leads, I believe in quantity versus quality when buying them. I will always buy 500 / 50 cent leads versus 100 one dollar leads for two simple facts.

Number one, when dealing with a lead broker, it's like a box of chocolates. You never know what you're going to get. (I hope I don't have to pay anyone a royalty for that last comment)!

Number two, I firmly believe that a good script (what you will say to these people) can conquer all. I have even purchased leads for 20 cents that allowed me to find and sign up 30 to 40 good people.

That's right, there is such a thing as 20 cent leads. In a minute I'll tell you how to find and purchase them.

I told you this book was full of tricks and strategies that could change the way you look at the network marketing industry forever.

At this point, we have covered warm market leads and lead brokers. The third way to create leads is by actually generating them yourself. You can do this a number of ways. I'm going to name just a few for now and will cover them in more detail in a later chapter entitled, "Generating Leads".

Below are just a few ways you can generate your own leads which you know are fresh.

- e-mail blasting
- auto-dialing
- blogging
- news groups
- small ads in magazines
- small ads in newspapers
- small ads on the internet
- small ads on MySpace
- small ads on Facebook
- Google AdWords

You will notice that most of the advertising venues mentioned above deal with small ads. Here's why - when you come up with a winning classified ad, which we will cover in a later chapter, the possibilities are endless.

Did you know that the National Enquirer tabloid has a place for business opportunity ads? TV Guide, which has a viewership of over 20,000,000, has a place for these types of ads as well. I think at one time TV Guide was even in the Guinness Book of World Records for the largest distribution of a weekly publication, and you can put your network marketing ad in it. Wow!

When you get to the chapter, "Generating Leads", you will truly understand that there are unlimited people out there who are ready and able to join your business. They will even call you!
Your primary job is to find these people using leads purchased from a broker, or leads generated yourself with advertising as quickly as you can. Remember the smiley face example? You are really sorting people, not selling.

I hope you can see that there are hundreds, if not thousands of lead brokers out there and 100,000 different places to run small print ads. That's not even including the use of internet or Google Adwords for finding new people to contact, which we will also cover in this book. When you look at it like this, I know you can see that finding 20 new people a day to introduce to your business is easy.

If you have been wondering how the people at the meetings who are making twenty to thirty thousand dollars a month do it, I hope you can see now that it all comes down to exposures, leads, and TRAINING! Here's what is great about being involved in a network marketing company. Along with a product or a service, you also offer the ability to make money from home. 98% of all people need to make more money. If you were to put 100 people in a room right now, 98 of them worry about money on a daily, if not hourly basis.

This takes into account the fact that only 2% of the United States is considered to be wealthy. This means that out of 100 people in that room only two of them do not worry about money.

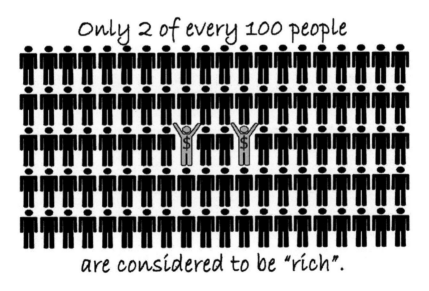

What does this mean? It's simple. Almost every person you come in contact with on a daily basis is a lead. WOW!!! Another great thing is the fact that most network marketing companies are almost 100% internet-based. What does this mean?

Since the birth of the internet, people have been fascinated with it and have been trying to figure out a way to make money online. Taking into account the fact that your network marketing company is internet-based means that the average person could be looking for exactly what you are offering. All you have to do is expose your product and business opportunity to them.

The law of averages will then take over.

It's really very simple. The more people you expose your business and product to, the faster your downline will grow due to the law of S-I-N-A-L-O-A. This stands for:

S-afety I-n N-umbers A-nd L-aw O-f A-verages.

A great example of this law of averages is a telemarketing room. We have all been called by them and will continue to be called by them for years to come for one simple fact. They generate sales! Let me tell you a short story so you can see exactly what I mean. I was speaking at an event in front of hundreds of people. I was explaining S-I-N-A-L-O-A (the law of averages).

I asked the audience of 300 people how many people in the last few months had been called by a telemarketer notifying them that their car warranty was about to expire? What happened then shocked even me. Almost every hand in the room went up and was followed by a roar of laughter. Everybody immediately understood the power of S-I-N-A-L-O-A.

The telemarketers selling these car warranties have absolutely no idea if the person they are calling even owns a car, let alone a car warranty. They are working off of the principle of the law of averages.
Think about it. If there are 20 telemarketers on staff who can make 100 calls in 15 minutes, and just one person out of those 100 buys an $800 car warranty, that means the company is making $3,200 an hour!

Since nearly every person in that meeting was called by this company, including myself, I believe that this telemarketing company is calling directly from the **phonebook.**

Speaking of calling out of the phonebook, I have one more quick story to tell you, so you really understand the power of averages. If you read my story at the beginning of this book you will remember at one point in my network marketing career I was so desperate I actually shot a 30-second television commercial to help me find people to join my business.

I need to tell you the full story, so you can truly understand the power of working through the numbers. At the time I shot this commercial, I was involved with a network marketing company that was selling long distance phone cards. Please bear in mind this was almost 15 years ago before I really understood what a lead was.

After I shot the commercial, I showed it to the owners of the network marketing company with whom I had recently become friends. These guys were wonderful people, but looking back I would have to say they probably didn't know what a lead was either. In any case, after they viewed the commercial, they liked it so much they played it at all of their meetings.

Once I got my groove and got comfortable with the incoming calls, I eventually fell into a routine that allowed me to recruit one to two people a day. I believe at that time the company had a little over 10,000 distributors, and I knew I had to be one of the top recruiters.

While having lunch one day with Darryl, one of the owners, the topic of recruiting came up. He wanted to thank me for the incredible job that I was doing. Even to this day, personally signing up one to two new people a day is big. In my arrogance, I made a comment about being the top recruiter for the company and asked who came in a close second.

At this time, I expected Darryl to tell me there was really not a close second. Imagine my surprise when he informed me that the top recruiting position each week was actually going back and forth between me and a 22-year old from Louisiana named Steve.

I was in shock! I immediately asked if he was using my television commercial. The reason I asked was because I offered to allow other reps the opportunity to use it as long as it was not in Texas.

Darryl replied, "No he's not using your TV commercial. We're not sure what he's doing."

Over lunch, we decided that it would be a good idea to offer to fly Steve, the 22-year old from Louisiana, in to tour the home office, and hopefully learn his system for recruiting one to two people a day.

The day that Steve was to arrive I made sure to get to the home office an hour early. I was lucky the network marketing headquarters was only 30 minutes from my home. I set up my laptop (considered new technology back then!) in the conference room that sat 14 people. You get the picture. At that time, I was setting up for a strategic game of chess to give and take information with this young man to find out exactly what he was doing.

When Steve walked into the conference room, my jaw nearly hit the floor. If you can imagine, I was standing at one end wearing a suit with my laptop open, ready to play my newest version of my TV commercial. At the other end was Steve wearing a baseball cap and slightly worn out high top sneakers. When he found out who I was - the distributor whom the company was making a big deal of because I had taken the time and money to shoot a TV commercial - he actually pulled out a camera and asked Darryl, the owner of the company, if he could take a picture of the two of us together.

I immediately realized that we would not be playing a game of chess this afternoon in that conference room, but rather we were two young entrepreneurs openly sharing our recruiting systems to genuinely help one another. We spent a few hours talking about what it took to produce and shoot a TV commercial.

I also revealed what I had been saying when people called in response to my TV commercial, and how I would excite them so much that they would sign up within 15 to 20 minutes of talking with me. I later found out that this is known as a script. Don't worry. You guessed it - we will cover scripts in a later chapter.

After sharing all of my tips, tricks, and scripts that allowed me to put one to two distributors in my business a day, it was now Steve's turn to share his system. By this time, both owners and the receptionist had joined us in the conference room. When we let Steve know that he was one of the top recruiters in the entire company, you could genuinely see a look of shock on his face. He could not believe that he was running neck and neck, sale for sale with the distributor who had filmed a TV commercial.

When we asked Steve what he was doing that allowed him to sign up one to two people a day, the answer that came left everybody in that room speechless, including me. Steve reached down into a beat-up leather briefcase and pulled out a residential telephone book from Louisiana.

Yes, a **telephone book** of Louisiana, his home state. He then proceeded to flip it open to the page he had most recently called. You could literally see the process that Steve used written right in the book next to each number. Steve had written "no", "yes", "conference call", or "call back" in the margin next to each person he had called.

He told us that, in his mind, this was simple. This is the best example of S-I-N-A-L-O-A (Safety In Numbers and Law of Averages) I could ever give you. When contacting people, he quickly realized that there was no faster way to go than the telephone. He also realized that he was not only offering a product, but the opportunity to make extra money from the comfort of your own home.

When he saw the telephone book, he said it was a no-brainer. He knew that most of the people in that telephone book needed to make more money, and he was dead on. Steve didn't realize that literally 98% of Americans worry about money on a daily basis. What he decided to do after joining the network marketing company, was commit to calling one full page of people out of the telephone book every single day.

He quickly realized he could call a full page in two to three hours a day. You could see from looking through all the previous pages called that he was steadily recruiting one to two, and in some cases, even three people a day for his network marketing business. I hope you can see the moral to the story. It all goes back to what I said at the beginning of this chapter. In most cases, the people who expose their product and business opportunity to the most people each day are the same people walking around the network marketing meetings making $20,000 to $30,000 a month. It's this simple. If you have a good script and are willing to pick up the phone and make no less than 20 exposures a day, then building a network marketing downline is easy.

Quick example: I want you to fold your arms right now; just cross them right in front of you. Wait 15 seconds. Unfold them, then fold them again in the opposite way from the first time you folded them.

It's a little hard to do and even a little uncomfortable, but does it hurt? NO! Did you break anything? NO! Well, that is exactly what picking up the phone and starting to call leads feels like. Is it fun? NO! The truth is, it is a little uncomfortable. The good news is once you get comfortable with it, it becomes no big deal.

Here's the great news. Chances are if you contact 20 new people a day for just 30 days, your telemarketing efforts should have your network marketing business up and moving on its own after one short month. Depending on how fast you can get your current downline to read this book and get trained, you could cut your 30 days of telemarketing down to 20 days.

Then you will move into a manager role. At this point, the best advice I can give you is that you have to treat your network marketing business as if you had to take a second mortgage out on your home to get your business started.

When you start a network marketing business for $200-$300, it is very easy to put your business in the hobby category rather than treating it like a true multi-million dollar business that can deliver $20,000 to $30,000 of income each month. I know that day in the conference room with Steve, he truly felt like he learned so much from me due to the fact that I took the time and energy to shoot a television commercial.

In actuality, the lesson about law and averages and making exposures that Steve taught me that day was priceless. I knew I had stumbled onto something big. I would eventually discover how big that lesson was. Six months later, I actually found myself in a professional telemarketing room consisting of over 100 employees.

I quickly realized that everything I learned in the conference room that day with Steve was just the tip of the iceberg.

When I got off the elevator and ended up in the middle of a room of 100 plus telemarketers, all talking at the same time and saying pretty much the same thing, it was the precise moment that I realized how important a good script and massive exposures are to any business.

This telemarketing room was selling a business opportunity that consisted of grocery coupon books. This room would make anywhere from $50,000 to as much as $200,000 in a single day.

What I want you to realize about this telemarketing room that earned as much as $200,000 in a single day is the simple fact that all these sales came from **leads, scripts**, and **exposures**.

You also need to know that when my friend Donny hired new telemarketers, they would literally spend the first week calling right out of a simple phonebook while they were getting comfortable with their new job and scripts.

You would be surprised to know that many companies use this strategy, including, pest control, auto dealerships, and so forth. I recently found out that stockbrokers have to make 400 calls a day right out of a phone book during their internship, which could last for 2 years or more.

Considering that I am only asking you to use this form of marketing for 30 days seems like a joke compared to a 2 year internship. At this point, you know that people are building companies, businesses, and network marketing downlines with the power of scripts, leads, and cold-calls. I want to tell you right now that everything you will learn and discover in this book I have done and continue to do to build my own personal network marketing business. My slogan when it comes to building my own personal business is: WHATEVER IT TAKES!

I am letting you know ahead of time that when starting this cold-calling process the phone will literally weigh ten pounds for the first 50 to 100 calls.

You will definitely be out of your comfort zone. Then something magical will start to happen. You will begin to get comfortable with your script, along with the process, and fall into a routine. When this happens, you will become very valuable to the network marketing industry because you now know how to expose the product and your business opportunity to the masses.

If you will recall, I was featured on a 30-minute television show and my name has appeared in handful of magazines. I even had a network marketing company offer to send a private plane to pick me up just to tour their home office. All of this is because I know how to make exposures, and by the end of this short book you will too! The good news is that once you have a sales team in place, you will slowly move into a management position.

This is when you will be able to slow down on the actual exposures that you make and start to guide your new distributors through the processes discovered in this book.

You will start out making as many exposures as possible, which will eventually turn into sales and sales people. After your sales team is in place and they have read this book, you will slowly move into the **Sales Manager** position. Eventually you will transition to **Manager/Partner,** and ultimately end up as **Retired Partner** in a network marketing company, receiving a residual income.

Keep in mind that when you build a distributorship in a network marketing company you actually OWN that position. When getting your company off the ground, your motto should be:
Whatever It Takes!

Before we move forward to the next chapter and begin to talk about leads and creating leads, we need to get organized and put our marketing tools in order. This involves the actual set-up of your binder. All you will need to do this is a simple 3-ring binder, some paper, and a pen.

Staying organized is key when you are going to be talking to 20 or more people on a daily basis. You will need to know where each new person/prospect is at all times in your recruiting process.

You will see what I mean when we set up your binder.

This may seem like a minimal process that you can skip, but I assure you it is of utmost importance. When I have helped people set up their binders at live meetings, I can't tell you how many people would come up to me after the training and thank me for making it so clear.

What I realized was people who join a network marketing business have a basic idea of what they need to do, but they don't know where to begin. Building the binder puts it all down in black and white.

You will see by the end of this short book how our binder and script will work hand in hand to help expose your network marketing product and business opportunity to the masses in the least amount of time.

Let's Get Started!

The first tab and page in your binder will be your Work Schedule. This is a simple page, as you can see by the picture below, but it performs a very important task. Remember, when starting a network marketing business, do not put this in the "Hobby" folder or the "I Just Joined a Club" file.

By actually writing down your work schedule each Saturday for the following week, it will set the foundation for a real business followed by a real work week. Every Saturday you need to sit down and review the upcoming work week. You will need to actually write in the days you plan to work, as well as the hours each day. You even go as far as determining how many exposures you plan to make on a weekly basis.

Please keep in mind, when you have a sales team of five, ten, or one hundred people in your network marketing business who have each read this book, they will also build the same binder that you are about to construct right now.

It could help create a virtual phone room in your downline, capable of making hundreds of exposures on a daily basis to help build your business.

Let's create Page #1 in our binder!

Work Week Schedule

Mon: 3 pm-6 pm   6:00 pm company webinar

Wed: 5 pm-7 pm   7:00 pm Live Company Call

Fri: 3 pm-6 pm   6:00 pm Live Company Call

Sat: 9 am - Live company training call

Our second page will consist of scripts. This page will be comprised of what you and your team will say on a daily basis when presenting your product and business opportunity to others. At this point, write the word "Scripts" at the top of the page, and you can return to this page to fill it in after we cover "Scripts" in a later chapter.

Let's create Page #2 in our binder!

Introduction Script

Example of an introduction script:

"John, this is _____ and I am calling you from my home office. I understand that you have responded to an ad about making money from home sometime in the last 30 days.
All I would like to do is play you a FREE video right over your computer that will reveal a secret home business that is making people incredible profits right from home. Only a small handful of people in the entire U.S. have seen the 3 minute video you are about to see. John, let me know when you're in front of your computer and I'll give you the website address and this call will be over. It's that simple."

The End

Building the third page in our binder will vary for each person who reads this book because there is no way I can know the exact marketing materials that your network marketing company provides.

What I must assume is that your company has some sort of online video explaining your product and business opportunity which may be played right over the internet. The next assumption is that you have a product or a service that you can demonstrate.

My recommendation is to talk to your upline, the person in your network marketing company who is recruiting the most people and making the most money, and ask them what marketing tools they are using.

Take the three best marketing tools your company offers and make these the first 1, 2, and 3 steps in your binder. I want to give you two examples of what this page may look like.

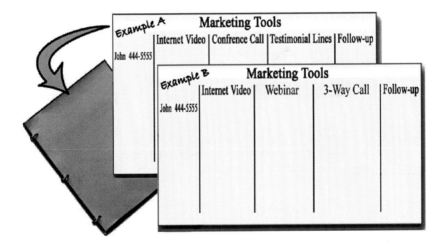

Example A	Marketing Tools			
John 444-5555	Internet Video	Confrence Call	Testimonial Lines	Follow-up

Example B	Marketing Tools			
John 444-5555	Internet Video	Webinar	3-Way Call	Follow-up

Remember, you need to pick the marketing tools which best represent your business opportunity. Once again, these marketing tools will vary from company to company and that is why I gave you the two examples shown above to demonstrate what your page may consist of.

If you're not sure which company marketing tools to utilize, just leave the columns blank for now.

Your binder will work hand in hand with scripts to move people from one marketing tool to the next, which brings them closer one step at a time to signing up in your business.

Let's see your binder in action.

In our example below, you can see that John, in our name column, watched our video and has also been on our conference call. The next step in our binder is to complete a 3-way call to our upline to help create excitement and urgency.

You will understand how important creating urgency (also called "the fear of loss") is when you get to the chapter on "Scripts".

Marketing Tools

	Internet Video	Conference Call	3-Way Call	Follow Up
John 444-5555	X	X		
Mary 222-4444	X			
Tom 444-2222				

You will notice from the example above that Mary only had time to watch the video and did not get on our conference call yet. She is followed by Tom, who as of now, we have yet to speak with.

As you can see, with this page in our binder, we will always know exactly where each person (lead) on our list is at all times.

When you have 25, 50, or even 100 people under your name column in your binder, this system of keeping track of everyone is very effective.

In fact, I can tell you that professional telemarketing rooms use a system very similar to this. Don't worry.

By the time you finish the chapter "**Generating Leads**", you will also learn how to fill the name column with as many names as you need to make 20 exposures a day.

You will truly understand that there are unlimited people out there who are ready and able to join your business, and they will even call you.

After completing the chapter, "Generating Leads", you will quickly realize that finding 20 new people a day to add to the list in your binder is almost a joke.

You should also be starting to see at this point that marketing and sales is a step by step process.

At this point, please keep in mind that all we are doing is setting up our binder. By the time you finish this book, you will know exactly what to say word for word every step of the way.

You will also know how to start a drip campaign, which we will use in all of our future follow-ups. By the time you finish this book, you will have no questions left unanswered.

Okay, let's set up our last page, which is a simple and gratifying page to create. You will see by the example on the next page that this page in our binder is dedicated to all the distributors we have personally sponsored into our business.

"This is called your "Frontline!"

(see example on the next page)

You will include their names, phone numbers, and email addresses, so their information will always be close and easy to find. You will want to communicate with them on a daily basis.

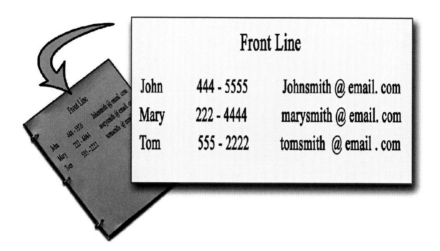

When you start to fill up this page with the names and e-mail addresses of your new distributors, you will notice that your job description will slowly shift from finding new business and distributors to more of a manager role, which will consist of keeping in touch with the leaders in your downline and helping them with anything they need to be productive and bring in new sales and sales people.

This brings up a very good point. I appreciate that you bought my book and with that I feel the least I can do is tell you the truth.
I hate when I hear other network marketers tell people that they are having so much pleasure building their businesses and how much fun it is to call strangers on the phone to try to get them to join their team.

That is one of the biggest problems with the network marketing industry. The fibs, and in some cases, flat out lies people use to try to get people to join their business is absurd.

Here's a fresh idea, considering that we are all grown-ups: why not give them a marketing system that absolutely works like the one contained in this book, and tell them the TRUTH on what they have to do over the next 30 to 60 days to be successful?

This way they can sit back, relax, and enjoy the fruits of their labor. The system you are about to discover really works.

If it is done correctly and given the attention it deserves, you could be finished in as little as 60, or even 30 days. I would like to point out that I said, "when you work the business correctly". My definition of working this system correctly all comes down to numbers.

The first 60 days of your new business should be spent making no less than 20 exposures a day. Using the binder we just created, along with leads and scripts, which we will learn about in a minute, you should be able to make 20 new exposures in about two hours a day.

Think about this. Most people spend two hours a day stuck in their car going back and forth to work.

Recall our slogan, "Whatever It Takes". If you can stay committed for 60 days and average 20 exposures a day, which can be done in two hours, chances are when you have completed this 60-day run you will have a team of 30 or so people in place. These will be people who have read this book and will understand what they need to do to do the same.

Your goal is to sign up no less than 30 people in the next 60 days. Think about this. The average telemarketer needs to create 20 sales every week just to keep from being fired. You only have to do it ONCE!

Once you have personally put 20 new people in your business, your career of telemarketing should come to an end. From that point on, your role will strictly be a leadership and management role.

Remember, the beauty of network marketing is that you progress as depicted below.

Sales Person
    → **Sales Manager**
        → **Manager**
            → **Retired with Residual Income**

When operating in your management role, you will simply go to the contact page in your binder and keep in touch with your leaders over the phone or via e-mail on a daily basis.

Your primary job, at this point, is to create excitement and motivation. Another big role of a manager is to merely pass information along such as company conference calls and events, and stories of success from other distributers.

When you become a manager with an active downline, you will probably have a good income testimonial. At this position, you will want to make yourself available for 3-ways and conference calls with your leaders.

I am sure you will agree that this is a very small price to pay to be able to work from home on a part-time basis while creating a full-time income.

The final step in building this binder is to get a piece of masking tape and clearly write "WHATEVER IT TAKES!", and stick it right on the cover.

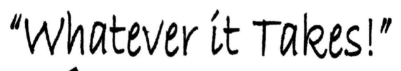

"Whatever it Takes!"

This will be our mantra for the next 60 days... failure is NOT an option.

Leave this binder in plain view as a friendly reminder that when building a network marketing distributorship, you need to be certain you are giving this business the attention it deserves.

At this stage we know it is possible, and I highly recommend that we fill up the name and number columns in your binder. First, start with your warm market leads.

A warm market lead is anyone you know who needs to make more money. Remember, you should be on a free long distance program, so you can call all over the country without costing you a dime. You should be able to come up with 30 to 40 names in your warm market.

Next, go online and purchase a few hundred leads from a lead broker. Remember what you learned about buying leads from brokers in this chapter. This should give you enough people to contact for 2 to 3 weeks.

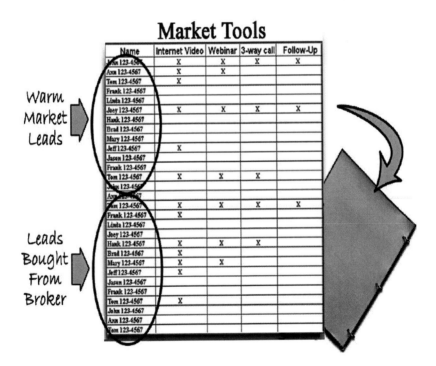

Market Tools

Name	Internet Video	Webinar	3-way call	Follow-Up
John 123-4567	X	X	X	X
Ann 123-4567	X	X		
Tom 123-4567	X			
Frank 123-4567				
Linda 123-4567				
Joey 123-4567	X	X	X	X
Hank 123-4567				
Brad 123-4567				
Mary 123-4567				
Jeff 123-4567	X			
Jason 123-4567				
Frank 123-4567				
Tom 123-4567	X	X	X	
John 123-4567				
Ann 123-4567				
John 123-4567	X	X	X	X
Frank 123-4567	X			
Linda 123-4567				
Joey 123-4567				
Hank 123-4567	X	X	X	
Brad 123-4567	X			
Mary 123-4567	X	X		
Jeff 123-4567	X			
Jason 123-4567				
Frank 123-4567				
Tom 123-4567	X			
John 123-4567				
Ann 123-4567				
Tom 123-4567				

Warm Market Leads

Leads Bought From Broker

Remember, for the next 60 days, you are going to try to average 20 exposures a day. You will be running through about 100 to 150 leads a week.

The next chapter will cover what to say and how to say it, so you can get the maximum return in the least amount of time from your leads. By the time you finish this book you will know exactly what to do, as well as what to say.

There will be no questions left unanswered. You will see exactly how to use a proven script, along with your binder, to get a new prospect (lead) to take a close look at your business opportunity.

If you are buying leads and using scripts, you are acting just like a professional telemarketer. This is called a campaign.

If you spend $150 on leads and the end result earns a $300 commission check from your network marketing company in addition to gaining new salespeople in your business, this is a SUCCESSFUL marketing campaign. You are definitely moving in the right direction.

After you cover the next chapter, "Scripts", you will be able to perform just like a professional telemarketer right from the comfort of your own home.

The average telemarketer with an average script will create one to two sales a shift, and you can enjoy the same numbers and sales right from home.

Remember Steve, the 22-year old guy from Louisiana whom I met over 15 years ago? He was calling people directly out of the telephone book and recruiting one to three people a day in his business, so you know it's possible.

Now, once again, you bought my book and I'm grateful. With that, the least I can do is tell you the truth. Telemarketing from home is absolutely not fun, but it is simple.

The good news is, if done correctly, you should be done telemarketing from home in the next 30 to 60 days. At that time, you should have a team in place who have all read this book and are now starting their 30 to 60 day run.

Once you have 10 to 15 people in your downline telemarketing from home to meet their goals of 20 exposures a day, you now have a virtual phone room working to promote your business. If you have two, five, or even ten people in your downline right now, the best thing you can do is have them go to

www.InsiderTellsAll.com

as soon as possible to get a copy of this book.

This one simple task alone can jump-start your business and bring dramatic results. At this phase, we just covered "outgoing calls", also known as cold calling.

By the time you finish this book you will also learn how it is possible to have strangers from all over the country calling you to find out more about your business opportunity.

These are known as "inbound calls" and when this happens you'll know that you're running a successful advertising campaign. The first time I received "inbound calls" I immediately realized there value and was actually able to personally recruit 5 to 10 people in a single day.

Remember, these were not just people; they were total strangers not friends or family. Before you get to excited about having a successful advertising campaign and "Inbound Calls" you need to slow down and use the system in this book and remember marketing is a process.

This book was written in such a way that you can realistically go to work immediately after you complete the next chapter, "Scripts", and EARN as YOU LEARN while you are putting the pieces in place to create your own lead capture system that will allow people to call you.

I have one tip left for you when it comes to buying leads. I told you that I have found a way to buy 50 cent leads for 20 cents. Here is how you do it. Lead brokers buy in bulk, and you can too.

Let's say a lead broker has offered to sell you 300 leads for $150 (basically 50 cents apiece).

If you can get that order up to let's say 3000 leads, 90% of the time you will get the same 50 cent lead for 20 cents. When you buy in bulk at Costco or Sam's club you save big.

The same applies when purchasing leads. Now, if you are saying, "Mike (that's me in case you forgot), that sounds good, but I don't have enough money to buy 3000 leads."

Here's how you do it. If you have a small downline in place, structure a bulk buy and split the leads. If you get a handful of people to go in with you, it's no big deal.

Here's the best part. Even if these leads are split up between 5 or 6 people in your downline, every lead who is contacted goes toward building your business. Additionally, you are helping your downline get cheap leads to help ensure their success!

Scripts

Knowing what not to say could be as important
as knowing what to say.

Insider Tells All Notes

I would like to start this chapter by simply explaining what a script is. You might not realize it, but you listen to scripts every single day of your life. Think about it.

When you watch a movie or television show, it all comes from a script. The very thing that allows some movies to win Academy Awards while other movies fail miserably at the box office all comes down to a winning script. Scripts are also what allow certain television shows like Seinfeld and Friends to appear year after year while other shows never even make it to prime time. Good scripts have even managed to find their way into American history books.

When JFK spoke the famous words, "*Ask not what your country can do for you but what you can do for your country*", that became one of the most famous quotes an American President has ever articulated. I'm here to tell you that famous quotes started as simple scripts written into speeches. At this stage, you should realize that scripts are all around us. The question is, how can we use them to help build our network marketing business? I promise by the time you finish this chapter you will have the answer to that question. A script is a really simple thing when you think about it. In a movie script, the lines are written so that Brad Pitt appears to say the perfect thing at the perfect time, so you come away from the movie thinking Brad is witty, funny, and cool.

Suitably, when writing a script to promote your business opportunity, instead of wanting a person to think you're witty, funny and cool, you want them to think your business opportunity is simple, fast, and easy. You want to paint the perfect picture by saying the perfect thing at the perfect time. The most successful salespeople around the world rely and work from proven scripts for the simple fact that a proven script creates sales. Whether you realize it or not, when you are building a network marketing distributorship you are a salesperson.

Remember in the last chapter we learned that for the next 60 days you will perform as a telemarketer from home using leads, your binder, and scripts to create sales.

At one time or another we have all been called by a telemarketer. Do you think those telemarketers are just saying whatever comes to mind, different things to different people each time? Absolutely not!

They are working from a proven script. They are saying the EXACT SAME thing to as many different people, as fast as they can, from one sale to the next. If you are working your business correctly, that is exactly what you should be doing.

I told you at the beginning of this book that the difference between making serious money in network marketing and making no money at all comes down to **exposures, exposures, exposures.**

When developing a script, the rules are fairly simple. You write your first draft, which I will show you how to do in a minute. Then you will slowly add and delete parts until you end up with a short, simple script.

Your script should get right to the point and most importantly, create sales. When you have the first draft of your script complete, it is time to go to work by getting on the phone and testing what you have created. Remember, a script is a work in progress. It will change as you get more comfortable with it, and when you open yourself up to making 20 to 30 calls a day. These small tweaks and little changes that you will make to your script along the way are no big deal.

It's easy. When you see that something you say to new prospects gets their attention or gets them excited, you keep it. When you say something that receives a negative response or creates a lot of questions and doubt, you simply delete it.

This process could take a few days or even a few weeks, but don't worry. While you are making these little changes to your script you are still exposing your business to new people and creating sales. While working on your script, you can **EARN AS YOU LEARN!**

Let me give you a quick example of what I'm talking about. At one point in my career, I was working with a network marketing company that was selling a business opportunity involving discount shopping software. I wrote the first draft of my script, so I could get on the phone and start exposing my new business opportunity to my warm market and some leads I generated with a few small ads. A good script always has an objective or goal in mind, as you will learn in a minute. My immediate goal with my new script was to get people to download my free discount shopping software.

The business opportunity was fairly simple to explain. A person would get my discount shopping software absolutely free and then would save money when they shopped online. I would then earn a commission on most of the products she purchased while using my software. This truly was a win-win situation for everyone.

If they liked my software and ended up signing up in my business, I would also earn commissions and overrides when they started to build their own business. My phone script up until this point was working like a charm. I would have a person download the free software, give them a quick demonstration of the software in action, then present them with the opportunity to become a distributor.

I had only been on the phone an hour, and had already given away a handful of free downloads. I even had a couple people sign up as distributors. Then, out of the blue, I ran across a particular person who was being difficult. You know the type.

I was already halfway through my script and, for whatever reason, this guy was not about to download my free software, let alone join my business. At this point, I decided to wing it for a second and say whatever came to mind to see if I could say something to create a little excitement or even the fear of loss to get this guy to download my free software.

Here's what came to mind, and this is what I said:

Script

"John, do you see that free download button on my website? If you hit that free download button right now and download my free software, I want you to think about this. At this point, you haven't bought anything, and I haven't sold you anything, but whenever you shop online with this discount shopping software this week, next month, or even next year, I could get a check. Now imagine if I give away hundreds of these free downloads."

That was all he needed to hear! I'm happy to say that John not only downloaded my software but he actually joined my business as a distributor and even went on to sign-up a handful of new distributors within his first few weeks in business. The name above was changed to protect the innocent.

No, but seriously, the statement shown above in bold was NOT in my initial script. However, it became a big part of that script, a real turning point for people who needed that extra little push. I consider it to be one of the strongest parts of the script and I stumbled across it in one conversation.

This is a great example of building on a script. In some cases, you might build on a script for days or even weeks. Good salespeople realize that sales are really based upon the art of persuasion. A good script can persuade a person to buy products, use your service, and join your business.

Realize most people whom I have run across in network marketing have never taken the time to write or develop a good script. What's worse is that most people in network marketing were never even told that a good script is the very foundation their new network marketing business will be built upon.

When you develop a script that creates sales, it will obviously help you get your business off the ground and create checks.

If you have a winning script getting good results, are you going to share it with your downline? Sure you are!

When you care about your downline's checks more than your own, your check will end up going through the roof. As you should see by now, a good script can make all the difference in the world.

What I have found in network marketing is that most people will join the business and not use scripts. They will say different things to different people off the top of their heads and will get inconsistent results. They will hear a handful of

"I'm not interested"

responses and then give up. They then become one of those people who walk around saying network marketing doesn't work or it's a scam.

The reason you will work from a script is simple. A good script is designed to get a new prospect to take action immediately. When a good script is used correctly, you will be able to walk a new prospect (lead) through two or three steps in your binder in one phone conversation.

Marketing Tools

	Internet Video	Conference Call	3-Way Call	Follow Up
John 444-5555	X	X	X	
Mary 222-4444	X			
Tom 444-2222				

When you have a list of people to call, be it your warm market or leads you purchased from a broker, and you have a script that gets results, it is called GAME OVER!

When you and your downline are working from a script that gets results like this, you are now working as a professional telemarketing room capable of making hundreds of exposures on a daily basis.

Exposures are the very thing that will allow you to build a network marketing distributorship in weeks instead of months or possibly years. If you are wondering why I keep referring to a telemarketing room when it comes to building a downline, it's simple. I have had the privilege of standing in the middle of one of the top producing telemarketing rooms in the country. I have personally watched this room sell over $200,000 in product in a single day.

By the way, that product was a business opportunity! I told you there are people everywhere ready and willing to join your business. You just need to find them.

When both you and your downline are working with leads and a proven script, you are working just like a professional telemarketing phone room. A telemarketing room can create massive sales and expose a product to the masses in a very short time. That is exactly what a downline can do when it is trained and running correctly.

The major difference between working as a telemarketer day in and day out and OWNING your own network marketing distributorship is simple. A telemarketer's work is never done. When you use leads and scripts to build your network marketing business, you will only have to use this aggressive form of marketing for a short time until your distributorship is established and growing on its own.

Remember, at the beginning of this book I told you one of the biggest problems with the network marketing industry is that you have people telling each other, "all you need to do is recruit two or three people and your job is done". The bad news is there really is no way to put a number on how many people you have to recruit to get your network marketing business established and growing on its own. It could happen with two or three sales, but I will tell you that I believe in safety in numbers.

Recruiting two or three people is definitely not playing it safe in my mind. I would say that you really need to focus on recruiting more in the range of 20 to 30 people in the next 30 to 60 days if you are serious about your network marketing career. The good news is when you are using scripts and leads like a professional telemarketer, you could personally recruit 20 to 30 people in as little as 30 days, possibly less. I have personally recruited 30 people, who were complete strangers, in 5 days a few times in my career.

That might sound crazy to you right now, but I am here to tell you that recruiting 30 people in 5 days is easy when you have a system in place. That is exactly what this book is introducing you to right now. Here's another way to look at it. The average telemarketers making $10 an hour have to close an average of ten sales a week just so they don't get fired. Furthermore, on every Monday they start all over again at one. They do this week after week and month after month. When I put it like that, the thought of having to make 20 to 30 sales TOTAL, just one time, seems like a joke doesn't it? Sure it does.

I want to give you one more example of what a good script is capable of producing to make sure you are in the right frame of mind before we get to the script writing part of this chapter.

Being in the right frame of mind is very important when writing a script. You need to know what is possible, so you see how big this really is.

Remember the story I told you about the car warranties? I would like to briefly recap that story because there is a point that needs to be made. I was training a large group of people about the importance of leads and scripts. I asked the audience how many people in the last 30 to 60 days had been called by a telemarketer informing them that their car warranty was up.

Out of an audience of 300 people, almost every single hand went up. That was quickly followed by a room of laughter. You might even have a smile on your face right now because you too have been called by the telemarketing room. I then asked the audience this simple question.

Do you think the telemarketer at the other end of the phone truly knew if your car warranty had expired, or for that matter if you even owned a car at all? Of course he didn't! I explained to the audience that the caller is from a telemarketing room with a winning script who is simply working off the law of S-I-N-A-L-O-A which stands for **Safety In Numbers And Law Of Averages**.

Somewhere along the line, the owner of the telemarketing room got the bright idea to come up with a script that revolved around people owning cars. One of the reasons this script is so powerful is the simple fact that 8 out of 10 Americans own a car. Basically, every single person they contact could be a potential buyer of their product.

This is the best form of attacking the masses when using a script that I could give you. Considering that almost every person in the audience, including myself, was called by the telemarketing room leads me to believe that these guys might be calling directly out of the phonebook.

Once again, what is allowing this company to do millions in sales by calling right out of the phonebook is the fact that 95% of Americans own a car.

You can't quote me on this, but I heard through the grapevine that this telemarketing room selling car warranties is doing about a million a month in sales, and it all started with a simple script.

Here is something I want you to think about, and this is where the light bulb should immediately go off over your head. The reason this particular telemarketing room is doing so well is because of its mass appeal, for the simple fact that 95% of Americans own a car. If you consider that only 2% of the United States is regarded as wealthy, this means 98% of the U.S. worries about money.

That sounds like mass appeal to me, what do you think?

Remember Steve, the young guy who was calling people right out of the phone book? I went through the trouble of shooting a TV commercial to find new contacts who needed to make extra money from home, while Steve simply picked up a telephone book and started calling page after page. The ironic thing about this is that we were both recruiting on average two people a day!

The difference is I was spending money to buy TV airtime which came directly out of my profits. Every time Steve signed a new person up out of the phonebook it was 100% pure profit because he was spending nothing to find new people to join his business.

This is a great example of what can happen when you have a product with mass appeal combined with a proven script that works. When I think back almost 20 years to the day I met Steve in that network marketing conference room, one thing comes to mind. At the time, I didn't know what a lead was, and I definitely didn't know the importance of the script. I can tell you this though. Steve made a handful of phone calls that day while we all watched, and I can definitely tell you that Steve said the exact same thing to all of the people he contacted.

I know Steve didn't realize it, but he was using a script. In fact, I'm not even sure that the owners of the network marketing company knew what a script was at that time. But I can tell you this: When Steve made phone calls and talked to new prospects, every person in the room, including me, wrote down what he said. You can't argue with success.

I will tell you right now on an average day Steve got 40 to 50 "NO's" from people for every "YES" that he got. Nevertheless, I would have to say when you are recruiting one or two new people a day into your network marketing business that sounds like a small price to pay.

Ask yourself this question right now: What would one to two new people a day mean to your network marketing business?

Don't forget, you only have to use this aggressive form of marketing to get 20 or 30 frontline people in your distributorship who have each read this book. At that time you will have a virtual telemarketing room making massive exposures to build your business. At this point, I hope you are in the right frame of mind and can clearly see the importance of having a script that performs and creates sales. When I told you a good script can MAKE YOU RICH, I meant it.

So let's get to it.

The main purpose for using a script is to get our new prospects to perform a certain way and most importantly, take immediate action.

A good script will create curiosity and fear of loss. A script is basically made up of four components. You have:

1. The Opening Line

2. The Introduction

3. The Body

4. The Close

Opening Line

Example of a GOOD opening line to a phone script: **"Hello John, this is _____"**

I know this seems extremely basic, but your opening line is where it all begins. Your opening line in the script, and how you deliver it, can literally make or break your advertising campaign.

I can't even count how many bad scripts I have seen over the years that start with a question and end up costing the person delivering the script hundreds of dollars a month in leads.

Let me take a moment and explain why starting your script with a question could end up costing you time, energy, and most importantly wasted money spent on leads. Say you call a lead you purchased from a broker. This particular lead was left by a person named John, and John happens to be the person who answers the phone when you call.

When you start your script with a question like

"Hello, is John available?"

John immediately knows that you are a stranger because you didn't recognize his voice.

John will immediately go into defense mode because he knows the person on the phone is a stranger and is probably going to try to sell him something. Think about it. How many times have you pretended to be someone else when a telemarketer called so you could get off the phone faster? Exactly.

When calling leads, always assume that the person picking up the phone is the person you are looking for. When John answers the phone and hears **"Hello John, this is _____."**, nine times out of ten he will reply with a simple "Yes". Congratulations. Mission accomplished. We now have the right person on the phone. This is your first goal when calling leads.

As simple and basic as this is, I felt we had to address it because it is that important. Think about it. Let's say you spent $100 for 50 leads, and you started your script with a question like **"Hello, is John available?"** If you were unable to get your prospect on the phone, the end result is wasted time, energy, and money spent on pointless leads.

The next part of the opening line simply states who you are. You will identify yourself, and then tell him why you are calling. This sentence will vary a little, depending on if you got the contact from a lead broker, or generated the lead yourself through advertising or other avenues which you will learn about in the chapter "Generating Leads".

IMPORTANT: In the following script, the sentence,

"I understand that you have responded to an ad about making money from home sometime in the last 30 days",

is what you will say when contacting the leads you have purchased from a BROKER. When you are contacting leads you have generated YOURSELF through ads and other avenues which we will cover in the chapter "Generating Leads", you will rephrase that sentence. When you contact leads you have generated yourself, you will say,

"Hello John, this is _____ and I am getting back with you. You left your name and number on my website and wanted me to contact you about a home business that only a handful of people know about at this time."

Okay, back to the script. Now, we need to meet our first goal and get our lead to watch our MLM video or listen to our MLM sizzle call. This is **VERY IMPORTANT**, first, try to get the lead to watch the video but if they are not in front of a computer you need to be ready to play them your sizzle call right over the phone.

Introduction Script

Example of an introduction phone script:

"John this is _____ and I'm calling you from my home office. You responded to an ad about making money from home sometime in the last 30 days. <u>All I would like to do is play you a 3 minute video right over your computer that will reveal a home business that is earning some people profits in their first 24 hours right from home.</u>

Only a small handful of people in the entire U.S. have seen the 3 minute video you are about to see. John, let me know when you're in front of your computer and I'll give you the website address and this call will be over. It's that simple."

The End

You will notice in the underlined portion of our introduction script shown above that I am saying something in the first 20 seconds that creates curiosity and fear of loss. At this point, I'm basically trying to say something that will entice John to stay on the phone. Most people don't remember calling or responding to an ad on the internet if it happened more than 24 hours ago. Considering most of the leads that you will buy will be 30 days old, I can almost guarantee that John doesn't remember the initial ad he called on, let alone, calling an ad at all. For this very reason, it is extremely beneficial to create curiosity and fear of loss within the first 20 seconds of the introduction script so he will stay on the phone. There are obviously other techniques you can use for the introduction of your script, but I have found that creating curiosity and fear of loss right at the beginning works best. Remember, we have one goal to accomplish with our introduction script: getting John to watch our network marketing video.

VERY IMPORTANT: Try to stay on the phone with your prospect while he watches the video, so you can go right into the next portion of your script once the video ends.

Let's take another look at our introduction script.

Example of an introduction phone script:

"John this is _____ and I'm calling you from my home office. You responded to an ad about making money from home sometime in the last 30 days. All I would like to do is play you a 3 minute video right over your computer that will reveal a home business that is earning some people profits in their first 24 hours

right from home. <u>Only a small handful of people in the entire U.S. have seen the 3 minute video you are about to see</u>. John, let me know when you're in front of your computer and I'll give you the website address and this call will be over. It's that simple."

The End

You will now notice in the underlined portion of our script that immediately after I create curiosity and fear of loss, I go right into the next portion of my script without pausing. The underlined portion of the script shown above will now tell John that this entire call will only last a total of three minutes and then it will be over.

This portion of the script is very important because, at this time, John is literally deciding whether or not to get off the phone or stay on and hear what I have to say. It is now a very simple battle going on in John's head: his desire to hang up the phone, or stay on the phone and discover a successful way to make money from home.

This is why I stated earlier that a good salesperson realizes the art of persuasion. We are using our script to persuade John into taking the first step which, in this case, is to watch our three-minute network marketing video.

Let's take one more look at our introduction script.

Example of an introduction phone script:

"John this is _____ and I'm calling you from my home office. You responded to an ad about making money from home sometime in the last 30 days. All I would like to do is play you a 3 minute video right over your computer that will reveal a home business that is earning some people profits in their first 24 hours right from home. <u>Only a small handful of people in the entire U.S. have seen the 3 minute video you are about to see</u>. <u>John, let me know when you're in front of your</u>

computer and I'll give you the website address and
_this call will be over. It's that simple__."_

The End

The last underlined portion of our introduction script is where we create
a little more curiosity and then deliver our call to action which, in this
case, is to go to our website and watch our three-minute network
marketing video that will show him a simple, fast, and easy way to
make extra money from home.

You can see on the underlined portion of the script above that I tell
John that only a small handful of people in the entire U.S. have seen
what he's about to see. You should create a little last minute curiosity
before delivering our call to action which in this case is, watching the
network marketing video. You can then see I immediately asked John
to tell me when he is in front of his computer.

What I'm about to tell you is absolutely one of the most important
things that you need to remember when writing a script. You will
notice in the introduction that not one time do I ask John a question.
When you ask a question, you are immediately giving up control of the
conversation.

Here's an example. If at any time I asked John a question it would
most likely go like this:

Question: *"John, is now a good time?"*

Answer: *"Actually, now isn't a good time."*

Question: *"Do you have a minute to talk?"*

Answer: *"No, I'm sorry I'm walking out the door."*

Question: *"Do you remember responding to an ad?"*

Answer: *"No, I don't."*

Question: *"Do you have access to a computer?"*

Answer: *"No, my internet is down right now."*

As you can see, when asking questions it is very easy to lose control of the conversation. All John has to say is "no, now is not a good time, I don't remember calling an ad, or my internet access is down at the moment" to end this phone call.

Remember, when delivering a script to your lead, you have a goal. In this case, we want John to take the first step in our binder and watch the video. Anything short of that is not acceptable. It is best to stay on the phone with your prospects while they watch the video so you can go right into the next part of your script when the video ends.

Does this mean if you call a lead and he does not watch your video during your first phone conversation that you throw out that lead? Absolutely not. We will address that in a moment when we get to our follow-up script.

Let's take one final look at our introduction script before we move on.

Example of an introduction phone script:

"John this is _____ and I'm calling you from my home office. You have responded to an ad about making money from home sometime in the last 30 days. All I would like to do is play you a 3 minute video right over your computer that will reveal a home business that is earning some people profits in their first 24 hours right from home. Only a small handful of people in the entire U.S. have seen the 3 minute video you are about to see. John, let me know when you're in front of your computer and I'll give you the website address and this call will be over. It's that simple."

The End

What I would like you to do now is simply repeat the introduction script above and time it with a watch. You will notice that you can deliver this introduction script in less than 30 seconds.

That's all the time it takes to expose your network marketing business to someone. Can you say,

Exposures, Exposures, Exposures?

Every time you repeat your introduction script to a new person (lead) and he watches your network marketing video, simply put a check next to his name in the video column in your binder. By the way, congratulations, because you just made an exposure!

Marketing Tools

	Internet Video	Conference Call	3-Way Call	Follow Up
John 444-5555	X	X	X	
Mary 222-4444	X			
Tom 444-2222				

The introduction is by far the hardest part of the entire script. This is where you are going to get the majority of your rebuttals and negative comments. The introduction script shown above is about 80% of what you will actually say in your conversation.

The remaining 20% of the conversation will be ad-lib. There has to be a little room in every script for conversation. Unfortunately, there is no way I can prepare you for that. Remember, this is where you will have to add and delete portions of your script to best suit the business opportunity you are promoting.

I also want you to know you are going to get a lot more people saying **"no, I'm not interested"** than saying **"yes, I want to know more"**. You will probably even get hung up on a few times and possibly hear a "don't call here again".

It's not personal. It's all a part of the business and anyone who is making $20,000 to $30,000 a month in network marketing has experienced it. I consider it a very small price to pay when you consider the freedom that residual income can deliver. Also, please keep in mind that you only have to use this aggressive form of marketing until you personally recruit 20 to 30 people. Out of those people, there will be a handful who will read this book and pick up the ball and run with it. That's all you need. Remember, the average telemarketer has to sell an average of 10 deals a week just to keep from being fired. It really puts everything into perspective when you look at it like that. After a person has completed watching your video, it is now time to get to the body of our script and get the prospect to commit to attending your live call or webinar.

Remember, the introduction portion was the hardest part of our script, the portion where we would have received the majority of our rebuttals. When you move on to the body of your script you will notice that your job is going to get a lot easier because your prospect has just watched your network marketing video. If the video has done its job, your prospect should be excited. The basic principle of the body of your script will be simple. Prove with documentation that this business opportunity is simple, fast, and easy. You want to paint the picture that everything is already in place for him to be successful. You are now going to see how your script works hand in hand with your binder to get a new prospect from your opening line to your closing script in three simple steps.

Let's move forward to the body of our script.

Body of the script

"Well John, I hope you can see that we have something special here. <u>The product, the business, and most importantly the system your business will run on is already in place for you</u>. This call is just about over. The last thing I'd like to do is invite you to our live call tonight. This is going to be an incredible

call. You'll get a chance to hear from "INCOME STORY". You really don't want to miss this call because you'll also hear from "PRODUCT STORY". Well this call is over, John. Thanks for your time. The last thing I want to do is call you tonight 10 minutes before the live call and give you a FREE access code so you can listen in."

The End

As you can see by the underlined portion of our script, we don't waste any time with our script. Right off the bat we are pointing out to John that this is a turnkey business. I literally tell him that the product and the system his business will run on are all in place for him. The most common question you will get is, "Do I have to do what you are doing right now?" The direct answer is, "Yes! But, if it is done correctly, you will only have to do it for about 30 days and then you will move to a management position". Tell John that you believe it's a very small price to pay for business ownership, not to mention residual income. Let's take another look at the body or script.

"Well John, I hope you can see that we have something special here. The product, the business, and most importantly the system your business will run on is already in place for you. <u>This call is just about over. The last thing I'd like to do is invite you to our live call tonight</u>. This is going to be an incredible call. You'll get a chance to hear from "INCOME STORY". You really don't want to miss this call because you'll also hear from "PRODUCT STORY". Well this call is over, John. Thanks for your time. The last thing I want to do is call you tonight 10 minutes before the live call and give you a FREE access code so you can listen in."

The End

Right off the bat you can see by the underlined portion that we are telling John that this is call is almost over. This will allow John to concentrate on what we are saying and not worry about how much longer we are going to keep him on the phone. You can see by the underlined portion of the script shown above that we have a goal and a call to action in place. This is where we will complete the other step in our binder and get our new prospect, "John", to commit to being on our live call or webinar. As you can see, the body of our script does not contain any questions. I am guiding and controlling the conversation every step of the way. Remember, when you ask questions you are giving up control of the conversation. Let's take another look at our script.

Example of the body of our phone script:

"Well John, I hope you can see that we have something special here. The product, the business, and most importantly the system your business will run on is already in place for you. This call is just about over. The last thing I'd like to do is invite you to our live call tonight . <u>This is going to be an incredible call. You'll get a chance to hear from "INCOME STORY". You really don't want to miss this call because you'll also hear from "PRODUCT STORY".</u> Well this call is over, John. Thanks for your time. The last thing I want to do is call you tonight 10 minutes before the live call and give you a FREE access code so you can listen in."

The End

As you can see by the underlined portion of our script, I treat each live call like a special that can't be missed. It's not what you say, but how you say it. I'm going to say this twice because it's just that important. When you are talking to a new person (lead), you have to promote each live call or webinar like it is a once in a lifetime event that cannot be missed. You will build excitement for each live call by telling two short stories. You will keep the message short and sweet.

You will need to tell the most powerful income testimonial you can. Use yours if you can. If you have not developed one as of yet, take one from the many testimonials you hear each night on the live call or webinar. You will repeat this process with a product testimonial.

Now at this point I must tell you that using another persons' income testimonial is good, but nothing competes with income testimonials you have created from your own experience. That is why you've heard me say several times in this book that getting a good 30 day income story of your own is very important to your success. The reason we will package our income and product testimonials into a short story is simple. Any good salesperson will tell you that

"Information tells, but Stories SELL."

At this point, it's very important to remember that you are in sales. Once again, the script above contains 80% of what your conversation will consist of. The remaining 20% will obviously be ad-lib and the stories you choose to tell. Let's take one final look at the body of our script before moving on to the close.

Example of the body of our phone script:

"Well John, I hope you can see that we have something special here. The product, the business, and most importantly the system your business will run on is already in place for you. This call is just about over. The last thing I'd like to do is invite you to our live call tonight. This is going to be an incredible call. You'll get a chance to hear from "INCOME STORY". You really don't want to miss this call because you'll also hear from "PRODUCT STORY". <u>Well this call is over John. Thanks for your time. The last thing I want to do is call you tonight 10 minutes before the live call and give you a FREE access code so you can listen in.</u>"

The End

By now I'm sure you can start to see the components that make up a tight format for a closed script that contains no questions. The last thing we will look at is our call to action. Remember, the entire purpose of the body of our script is to get our new prospect to our live conference call or webinar.

As you can see by the underlined portion of the script above, we are putting John at ease by letting him know this call is over. We simply thank him for his time, then inform him that we will be calling him 10 minutes before our live conference call to give him a free code. When John agrees to attend your live call or webinar, simply put a checkmark in the column of your binder that says live call. I hope you can see at this point exactly how our script is working hand in hand with our binder to present our business opportunity to as many people as we can in a reasonable amount of time.

Marketing Tools

	Internet Video	Conference Call	3-Way Call	Follow Up
John 444-5555	X	X		
Mary 222-4444	X			
Tom 444-2222				

We have several things going on right here that I think you will find amusing. We've just put John at ease by telling him this call is now over. We then immediately follow up by letting him know that we will call him with our free access code.

The first thing you will notice is that I did not ask John if he had time to attend my call. You will also notice that I didn't ask John if he would like to attend my call.

I'm going to assume that John is excited about the business opportunity, and after hearing my short product and income stories that he can't wait to attend the call. We have one last trick up our sleeves. This trick alone is worth the full price of this book. I have learned throughout the years not to give a person my conference call number or webinar address at three o'clock if my call or webinar does not take place until eight o'clock.

The simple fact is that nine out of ten people will forget about your call or will misplace your phone number. If that happens, everything you have done has been a waste if the person does not attend your live call or webinar. I have found the system that works best is to get a handful of people to commit to attending your call and then call them 10 to 20 minutes before each live call. This will be a short, one-minute phone call in which you simply give, in this case John, the phone number and access code, along with a simple one-line sentence that creates a little excitement. All you need to do is simply repeat a short income testimonial from a person who will be on the call tonight.

THIS IS VERY IMPORTANT. When building your distributorship, you will work the phones your absolute hardest 30 minutes prior to each call or webinar. You want to make sure every person in your binder who has agreed to be on your live call or webinar has the correct phone number and access code or webinar address.

Don't forget to deliver one or two simple sentences at this time to create a little excitement and fear of loss to help assure that they make it to the call.

THIS IS VERY, VERY IMPORTANT. The technique I'm about to share with you can literally be the difference between recruiting one or two people a week, versus five or six. What we will do before each live call is now pick our "best prospect", the person you think is most likely to join your business, and call him two minutes before our live call. We will not give our best prospect for the day the phone number and access code. Instead, we will 3-way directly into the call personally. This is a very simple process.

You merely call your best prospect for that day. You will tell him to hold on, then click over using 3-way on your phone and call directly into the live conference call. This simple technique will ensure that you have at least one new prospect on each call. If you are using a webinar instead of a live call, you talk to your best prospect for that day real-time until he is logged-in to the webinar. When using the "Insider Tells All" recruiting system in this book, you will work your hardest 30 minutes before each live call or webinar by contacting all the new prospects on your list who agreed to participate. You will give them the live call phone number and access code or webinar address. Immediately after the live call ends, you will call back each new prospect who participated to repeat the close of your script shown below.

This by far is the most important part of our script. It is where a sale is going to take place. You are either going to sell your new prospect on the idea of joining your business, or he is going to sell you on why he can't. Either way, a sale is going to take place. As you will see, this is why in the close of our script we will pull out all the stops. At this point, you will get him to complete the third and final step in your binder which will either be a 3-way call to your upline or a 24-hour testimonial line.

Remember, you pick the marketing tools that you feel work the best. If your upline (the person who signed you up) has a good income or product testimonial you can use him for the 3-way as the last step in your binder. If your network marketing company supplies a good 24-hour testimonial line, you may choose to use that. Either way, in the close you will pull out all the stops.

Let's get to it.

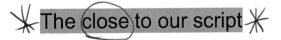

The close to our script

Example of the close to our phone script:

"Hello John. I wanted to make sure that you were on the call in time to hear the incredible testimonial from_____? John, I want you to hear from one more person who is in this business. This will only take a minute. Please hold on."

91

"John, what I would like to do is go ahead and get you in the business and get your website online right now. It's only $$$$, and that covers everything you need, including the product and your very own website. Now, if I were you, I would use a credit card to sign up just like I did. Then we will focus on making $1,000 in commissions in your first 30 days!

Even if we fall way short of that goal, I think the worst case is, we will still cover your investment of $$$ before your credit card bill ever comes in. From that point on, everything is pure profit.

I want you to know I'll be here every step of the way to help ensure your success. I'm even going to take it a step further and invest my own money in your business. Here's what I'm going to do. If you get started right now, I'm going to give you two FREE gifts that I'll pay for right out of my own pocket. The first FREE gift is a copy of the "Insider Tells All" book. This book alone retails for $24.95 and actually gives you step by step instructions on how to build this business.

The second gift I'll give you is 10 names and phone numbers (leads) of people who have already responded to an ad about making money from home. All you have to do is call them back and follow the step by step instructions in the "Insider Tells All" book that I'm following. It's really a simple system.

Think about this, John. Out of those 10 names and phone numbers I'll give you for FREE, if we just get (?)

*people in the business, your distributorship was 100%
free. Sound good? Great!"*

The End

Right off the bat, you will notice that our closing script is a little bit
longer than the other parts of our script. This is because we need to
pull out all the stops in our close to create the sale. If you read the
entire script through, it is really only about 60 seconds long. Once you
have read it 10 to 20 times you will actually have it memorized, which
is very important. You will see why I say that in a minute, but first, I
would once again like to break down the script line by line so you can
see the psychology and content that makes up a good script. As we
break this script down, I will only refer to the underlined portions, so
you don't get confused.

Example of the close to our phone script:

**"Hello, John. I wanted to make sure that you were on
the call in time to hear the incredible testimonial
from _____? John, I want you to hear from one
more person who is in this business. This will only
take a minute. Please hold on."**

(3- way to up-line) or (24 hour testimonial line)

**"John, what I would like to do is go ahead and get you
in the business and get your website online right now.
It's only $$$$ and that covers everything you need,
including the product and your very own website.
Now, if I were you, I would use a credit card to sign up
just like I did. We will then focus on making $1,000 in
commissions in your first 30 days! Even if we fall way
short of that goal, I think the worst case is, we'll still
cover your investment of $$$ before your credit card
bill ever comes in. From that point on everything is
pure profit.**

I want you to know I'll be here every step of the way to help ensure your success. I'm even going to take it a step further and invest my own money in your business. Here's what I'm going to do. If you get started right now I'm going to give you two FREE gifts that I'll pay for right out of my own pocket. The first FREE gift is a copy of the "Insider Tells All" book. This book alone retails for $24.95 and actually gives you step by step instructions on how to build this business. The second gift I'll give you is 10 names and phone numbers (leads) of people who have already responded to an ad about making money from home. All you have to do is call them back and follow the step by step instructions in the "Insider Tells All" book that I'm following. It's really a simple system.

Think about this, John. Out of those 10 names and phone numbers I'll give you for FREE, if we just get (?) people in the business, your distributorship was 100% free. Sound good? Great!"

The End

As you will see by the underlined portion in the script above, we begin by simply asking if they made it on the call in time to hear the incredible testimonial from_____. This little technique is allowing us to start our closing script on a positive note. Then you will notice that we go right into our last call to action which is our 3-way call to our up-line or our 24 hour company testimonial line. This will allow us to squeeze in one more income or product testimonial to help create the fear of loss while adding credibility to our business opportunity. Just imagine if you were on the call with two people at the same time who were both involved in the business opportunity and making money. This is what I mean by creating the fear of loss. After you complete the last step in your binder, simply put a checkmark in the column that reads three-way call or 24-hour testimonial line, depending on which tool you choose to use. Remember, you pick the tools that your company offers which are best for you. For this example, I will assume you are using a 3-way call.

Marketing Tools

	Internet Video	Conference Call	3-Way Call	Follow Up
John 444-5555	X	X	X	
Mary 222-4444	X			
Tom 444-2222				

I am sure at this point you can see how we used a simple script to walk our new prospect through the marketing steps in our binder. It is now time to create the sale and put a new person in our business. Let's take another look at our closing script.

Example of the close to our phone script:

"Hello, John. I wanted to make sure that you were on the call in time to hear the incredible testimonial from_____? John, I want you to hear from one more person who is in this business. This will only take a minute. Please hold on.

(3-way to up-line) or (24 hour testimonial line)

"John, what I would like to do is go ahead and get you in the business and get your website online right now. It's only $$$$ and that covers everything you need, including the product and your very own website.

95

Now, if I were you, I would use a credit card to sign up just like I did. We will then focus on making $1,000 in commissions in your first 30 days! Even if we fall way short of that goal, I think the worst case is, we'll still cover your investment of $$$ before your credit card bill ever comes in. From that point on everything is pure profit.

I want you to know I'll be here every step of the way to help ensure your success. I'm even going to take it a step further and invest my own money in your business.

Here's what I'm going to do. If you get started right now I'm going to give you two FREE gifts that I'll pay for right out of my own pocket. The first FREE gift is a copy of the "Insider Tells All" book. This book alone retails for $24.95 and actually gives you step by step instructions on how to build this business.

The second gift I'll give you is 10 names and phone numbers (leads) of people who have already responded to an ad about making money from home. All you have to do is call them back and follow the step by step instructions in the "Insider Tells All" book. It's really a simple system. Think about this, John. Out of those 10 names and phone numbers I'll give you for FREE, if we just get (?) people in the business, your distributorship was 100% free. Sound good? Great!"

The End

The underlined portion of the script above is where we will actually start our close. You will notice that I am not asking John if he would like to join my business. Remember, we have to stay away from

96

questions. If you ask a question, you might not get the answer you're looking for. I am assuming that after all the documentation and testimonials John has heard, he is more than ready and willing to join my business. What I am doing is a very old sales technique referred to as painting John into the picture of owning his own business. At this point, if John is not going to join my business he is going to have to tell me "no", which can be hard for some people to do.

Believe it or not, if John has been on a live call with you and then a 3-way, he feels a certain sense of obligation. It's not as easy as you would think at this point to simply say, "No, I'm not interested" when you have already painted him into the picture. As simple as this technique is, it could be the difference between making a sale or not.

The last thing we will do in this portion of our script is give him the price and point out that everything from the product to his very own website is included in the start-up cost. Make a note of this point. From what John has seen and heard that should be obvious, but it never hurts to point it out one last time. Let's take another look at our closing script.

Example of the close to our phone script:

"Hello, John. I wanted to make sure that you were on the call in time to hear the incredible testimonial from_____? John, I want you to hear from one more person who is in this business. This will only take a minute. Please hold on."

(3- way to up-line) or (24 hour testimonial line)

"John, what I would like to do is go ahead and get you in the business and get your website online right now. It's only $$$$ and that covers everything you need, including the product and your very own website.
<u>*Now, if I were you I would use a credit card to sign up just like I did. We will then focus on making $1,000 in commissions in your first 30 days! Even if we fall way short of that goal, I think the worst case is, we'll still*</u>

*cover your investment of $$$ before your credit card
bill ever comes in. From that point on, everything is
pure profit.*

*Now, I want you to know I'll be here every step of the
way to help ensure your success. I'm even going to
take it a step further and invest my own money in your
business.*

*Here's what I'm going to do. If you get started right
now I'm going to give you two FREE gifts that I'll pay
for right out of my own pocket. The first FREE gift is a
copy of the "Insider Tells All" book. This book alone
retails for $24.95 and actually gives you step by step
instructions on how to build this business.*

*The second gift I'll give you is 10 names and phone
numbers (leads) of people who have already
responded to an ad about making money from home.
All you have to do is call them back and follow the step
by step instructions in the "Insider Tells All" book that
I'm following. It's really a simple system.*

*Think about this, John. Out of those 10 names and
phone numbers I'll give you for FREE, if we just get (?)
people in the business, your distributorship was 100%
free. Sound good? Great!"*

The End

At this point, we are getting into the heart of our close. You will notice
that I am even going as far to suggest a form of payment, but I am also
telling him that this is exactly what I did. This simply points out that I'm
not asking John to do anything that I haven't already done. For some
people, this portion of the script where they are asked to pull out their
credit card could be viewed as negative.

It is very important to point out two or three positives for every negative, and that's exactly what we are about to do. You will notice directly after I request that he put his business on his credit card, I suggest that we shoot for $1,000 commissions in his first 30 days.

I merely point out if we get to work immediately we should be able to pay for our business opportunity with the commissions that we have received before our credit card bill ever comes in. You will notice I am still staying with the theme that John is planning to join my business. At this point, we are simply deciding on a method of payment.

Let's take another look at our closing script.

"Hello, John. I wanted to make sure that you were on the call in time to hear the incredible testimonial from_____? John, I want you to hear from one more person who is in this business. This will only take a minute. Please hold on."

(3- way to up-line)

"John, what I would like to do is go ahead and get you in the business and get your website online right now. It's only $$$$ and that covers everything you need, including the product and your very own website. Now, if I were you I would use a credit card to sign up just like I did. We will then focus on making $1,000 in commissions in your first 30 days!

Even if we fall way short of that goal, I think the worst case is, we'll still cover your investment of $$$ before your credit card bill ever comes in. From that point on everything is pure profit.

<u>I want you to know I'll be here every step of the way to help ensure your success. I'm even going to take it a step further and invest my own money in your</u>

business. Here's what I'm going to do, If you get started right now I'm going to give you two FREE gifts that I'll pay for right out of my own pocket.

The first FREE gift is a copy of the "Insider Tells All" book. This book alone retails for $24.95 and actually gives you step by step instructions on how to build this business. The second gift I'll give you is 10 names and phone numbers (leads) of people who have already responded to an ad about making money from home. All you have to do is call them back and follow the step by step instructions in the "Insider Tells All" book that I'm following. It's really a simple system.

Think about this, John. Out of those 10 names and phone numbers I'll give you for FREE, if we just get (?) people in the business, your distributorship was 100% free. Sound good? Great!"

The End

At this portion of the underlined script, it is time to give John some reassurance that he is in business for himself but not by himself.

You will do this by telling John that you will actually invest your own money in his business. Actions speak way louder than words, and the action of you investing in John's business might be the very thing that gets him to commit and sign up as a distributor. We will do this in the form of two free gifts John will receive which you will pay for directly out of your pocket. We have all heard the famous saying in advertising: "but wait - there's more!" The reason you have seen this technique used for the last 40 years and will continue to see it for 40 more is simple.

It works! Here's the good news. The gifts you will be giving John will actually help build his business and increase your check at the same time. The first gift you will give him is a copy of the "Insider Tells All" book. This book is the system his business will run on.

If he uses the system in the book to sign new distributors just as you are doing, this is called duplication. Duplication is the very thing that creates the $10,000 and $20,000 monthly commission checks in network marketing.

Before we go any further, let me tell you right now that you can go to InsidersMLMsecrets.com to purchase the "Insider Tells All' book for $5.00 each. That's an 80% SAVINGS! This is a great gift to give John because he can clearly see the retail price of $24.95 on the back. The InsidersMLMsecrets website, where you can order this book for $5.00, will also reveal another recruiting secret that will leave you speechless.

The next free gift that John will receive is 10 of the leads you purchased from a lead broker.

Remember, the goal we are trying to reach is a virtual telemarketing room. Can you think of a better way to do that than handing someone the "Insider Tells All" book that you are reading right now and a list of names and numbers to call on the same day they join your network marketing business? I told you at the beginning of this book that this is a 100% REAL system with auto-training built right in. You are being trained on the system, and part of that is training your downline with the same tools.

I know, I know, I'm a genius!

Let's take one last look at our closing script.

"Hello, John. I wanted to make sure that you were on the call in time to hear the incredible testimonial from_____? John, I want you to hear from one more person who is in this business. This will only take a minute. Please hold on."

(3-way to up-line) or (24 hour testimonial line)

"John, what I would like to do is go ahead and get you in the business and get your website online right now. It's only $$$$ and that covers everything you need, including the product and your very own website. Now, if I were you I would use a credit card to sign up just like I did. We will then focus on making $1,000 in commissions in your first 30 days!

Even if we fall way short of that goal, I think the worst case is, we'll still cover your investment of $$$ before your credit card bill ever comes in. From that point on everything is pure profit.

I want you to know I'll be here every step of the way to help ensure your success. I'm even going to take it a step further and invest my own money in your business.

Here's what I'm going to do. If you get started right now I'm going to give you two FREE gifts that I'll pay for right out of my own pocket. The first FREE gift is a copy of the "Insider Tells All" book. This book alone retails for $24.95 and actually gives you step by step instructions on how to build this business.

The second gift I'll give you is 10 names and phone numbers (leads) of people who have already responded to an ad about making money from home. All you have to do is call them back and follow the step by step instructions in the "Insider Tells All" book that I'm following. It's really a simple system.

__Think about this, John. Out of those 10 names and phone numbers I'll give you for FREE, if we just get (?) people in the business, your distributorship was 100% free. Sound good? Great!__"

The End

As you can see, we will close our script with one final positive note. We simply point out that, if we sign up just (?) out of the 10 names and phone numbers that you will give John, that his business is now 100% free!

John should clearly be able to see that you are giving him everything he needs to succeed. By the way, you are! The reason there is a question mark by the amount of people that John will need to sign up to break even is because each network marketing company is different, and there is no way I can know what it takes for your specific company. At this point, we have explained to John that there is absolutely nothing for him to figure out. We have a product, a business, and most importantly, a marketing system to run on. The very last thing we will address in our closing script is the final call to action by simply asking John if everything sounds good. If John replies with a "yes, okay, let's do it, I'm ready", basically any phrase that is remotely positive, this means that you just created a sale and put a new distributor in the business. At this moment, do not hesitate. Take John right to your network marketing website and sign him up while you're on the phone with him.

DO NOT leave it up to chance and hang up the phone in hopes that he will go through the sign up process on his own at a later date. However, if John hesitates, you instantly go to work. This is what being a closer is all about.

This is where your belief in your product and business opportunity needs to shine through. Remember, at this point, you have given John adequate time and documentation to prove that this business is real. The one thing I remember so clear about being in a professional telemarketing room was the sheer competence of the people working the phones. If John hesitates about signing up, you need to ask him a few of the following questions.

Rebuttal Script

"John, I want to ask you a question. You can see that this business is real, and real people just like you are making big money. What is holding you back from starting your business right now?"

The End

With the short script above, we are getting right to the point. We have no more time to waste. We need to know what is holding John back from signing up. Once John answers the question, we will then know what we are up against. If John replies that he likes the business opportunity that you have presented, but his money is tight at this time, he might actually be looking for a little reassurance. Here is a great example of what you should say.

Rebuttal Script

"John, if money is really that tight, then you need to start this business now more than ever. Don't forget, if we get started right now, your new website can be online in minutes ready to take orders and your two free gifts will be in the mail tomorrow morning."

The End

The example script above is a gentle push in the right direction and in most cases, believe it or not, that little push could be all that stands between you and a new distributor.

The biggest mistake I see time and time again in network marketing, and even professional telemarketing rooms, is the salesperson does not ask for the sale.

At this point, if John is adamant on not signing up that night, we simply move to the next column in our binder entitled "follow-ups".

There really is no script for the follow-up column, just seven simple words that you need to keep in mind.

"The Fortune Is In The Follow Up!"

When John has been through all the steps in your binder and has not said "yes" to your business opportunity, but he has not said "no", you need to put a checkmark next to his name in the follow-up column.

Marketing Tools

	Internet Video	Conference Call	3-Way Call	Follow Up
John 444-5555	X	X	X	X
Mary 222-4444	X			
Tom 444-2222				

You now know exactly where you stand with this lead, John. Remember, this business all comes down to numbers. In the chapter on leads we have already covered that a lead is a name, phone number, and if possible, an e-mail address.

If the leads you purchased or generated did not come complete with an e-mail address you need to ask John if you can have his e-mail address, so you can send him a few updates on this opportunity over the next 30 days. If he seems hesitant, just let him know it is your personal address book, and he can cancel at any time.

His e-mail address will come in very handy when using follow-ups to build your business. This process is extremely simple. At the end of each day, simply take all of the names in your follow-up column of people who did not sign up and add them to one specific group in your e-mail address book.

This simple technique will allow you to type out one e-mail and send it to multiple people with a simple click of a button. When using this technique to do follow-ups, keep one thing in mind: 98% of Americans worry about money on a daily, if not hourly basis.

You may have found the right person to join your business, but just caught them at the wrong time. Now that you know you can push one button and send out multiple or even hundreds of e-mails at one time, your mission is simple. Three times a week, send your follow-up list a short but powerful e-mail.

The three major topics your e-mails will consist of are: income testimonials from you and other people in the entire network marketing company, product testimonials from you and other people, and how simple and easy it is to run this business.

For the income and product testimonials, you can go outside your downline and use the BEST of the BEST testimonials in the entire company. You will usually be able to find your best testimonials on the live company calls or their 24-hour testimonial line.

When looking for guidance in writing good follow-up emails, make sure to use the principles and techniques discussed in the chapter, "Writing a Winning Ad".

Very important; In every follow-up e-mail you send, regardless of its income or product testimonials, always include a GREAT headline and your personal phone number as well as the conference call number to your next live call.

This simple technique is referred to as a "drip campaign". This form of marketing can produce phenomenal results with the simple click of a button. Not to mention, it's free.

Once you have created 7 or 8 good follow-up e-mails for your drip campaign, save them in a folder on your computer. This will save you a lot of time and work in the future.

When it is time to send out an e-mail to your follow-up list, simply cut and paste one of the 7 or 8 emails you have saved and hit send. We have just covered an important step that 98% of network marketers never do: FOLLOW - UPS.

You now understand what a winning script consists of and have an excellent first draft to work from. Simply take the outline of the script in this book and make it your own.

Tweak and change what you need to best fit the network marketing business you are currently promoting. Just remember to stick to the basic principles we covered in this chapter when you are changing up the script to best suit your needs.

Please remember that with any script, it is basically a guideline to follow. What I mean by that is 80% of your conversation with a new prospect will come from your script, and 20% will be improvisation and ad-lib.

One other important thing to remember when delivering your script is that it is not just what you say, but HOW you say it. If a person can hear that you are not excited or that you do not have total belief in your product, you might as well hang up the phone.

That's why I stated earlier that it is important to memorize your script as soon as possible. If you sound like you are reading, that is a fast way to get hung up on. I'd like to give you one more piece of advice before we move on to the next chapter.

With any good script you will have a goal and objective in mind. However, please remember to allow your new prospects an opportunity to talk and tell you what *their* objectives are as well when discussing your business opportunity.

Some of the BEST sales people are also great listeners. That is no accident.

They have learned along the way that sometimes the sale is actually made when your mouth is shut. This is why I have talked several times in this chapter about the 80/20 rule.

80% of your conversation will follow the script and 20% will allow your prospect to talk and ask questions to tell you what is on his mind.

I hope you can see after completing this chapter that building your network marketing business is all about exposures. Making exposures is easy when you have people to talk to, and even easier when you know what to say.

Generating Leads

Stop looking for a Big Hitter and become one.

Insider Tells All Notes

Before we jump into lead generation, I want to clearly explain why we want to generate leads. It all goes back to our binder.

It doesn't matter if we have warm market leads, leads purchased from a broker, or leads generated ourselves with small ads or other avenues - every name will go directly into our binder so we can put each person through the step by step marketing tools. The steps in our binder do not change. Generating leads simply gives us more people to talk to.

Market Tools

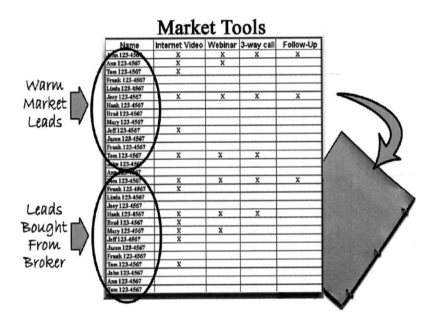

Here is the good news. Many of you who read this book and follow the simple instructions using your warm market leads & leads purchased from a broker will meet your goal of 30 personal recruits without ever having to place a single ad or generate leads on your own.

Remember, our immediate goal is to recruit 30 new distributors in the next 30 to 60 days and then put a copy of this book in their hands so they can do the same.

Duplication is the real power, and where most of the money comes from in network marketing. The beauty of this book is it will train your downline to duplicate without you saying one word.

Recruiting 20 to 30 new distributors can absolutely be done solely with leads from a broker and warm market leads. Remember, Steve the 22 year old did it with a plain old phonebook.

He recruited 20 to 30 new distributors in his first month because he was not afraid to pick up the phone.

I want to point out that he did not have to generate additional leads to be successful, just like you do not. However, when writing this book, I wanted it to appeal to both the person who is just trying to make an extra $2,000 a month, and at the same time, appeal to the advanced internet marketers who are trying to make a six figure income and personally recruit one to two hundred people themselves.

I want to go over just eight simple ways to generate leads. Any one of the eight advertising avenues shown below has the power to deliver incredible results when you have an ad campaign which allows you to break even.

Breaking even simply means earning back the money you invested. If you spend $500 on advertising and you make $500 in commission from your network marketing check, you are breaking even.

Your bonus is all the new sales people and distributors you now have in your business to help increase your check the following month. We will have more on that in a minute.

Let's get to it. I would like to begin by talking about just a few of the ways you can generate leads.

#1 Lead Brokers

The first and most reliable way to find new contacts is by dealing with a lead broker. You can simply go to Google or Yahoo and use the search terms,

home business leads
business opportunity leads
network marketing leads

Home Business Leads

These simple search terms should bring up hundreds, if not thousands, of lead brokers to choose from.

When buying leads, there really is no way of telling what you are going to get. Lead brokers usually divide leads into two separate categories, with the first being the actual time they say the lead was collected. The more recent the lead, the more money they will want for it.

The second category is referred to as "one-hit", "two-hit", or "three-hit" leads. This simply means that this list of contacts has already been sold to other people and passed around or circulated. One-hit means it was sold one time. Two-hit means it was sold twice, and three-hits obviously were sold three times.

My opinion and recommendation when purchasing leads is to always go for quantity versus quality for the simple reason that you never really know what you are getting in the first place. I also believe a good script can turn an old lead into a new distributor.

Therefore, when dealing with a broker, allow him time to give you his full pitch, then politely respond that you weren't planning on spending that much money. Ask if he has anything in the price range of $.25 per name. More often than not, he will always be able to dig up a list of people interested in making money from home. What I like about this method of lead gathering is, it's simple, easy, and most importantly, it's fast. You can purchase names and numbers today, and be on the phone immediately.

Quick tip: If you have 4 or 5 people in your downline who are serious about their businesses, you need to pull your money together to buy leads in bulk. This will give you more buying power because you are spending more money, and the lead broker will take you more seriously.

This will also help ensure that you get a good price because you are buying in volume. A downline of 5 to 10 people could put together $1,000 for leads instead of $100, and this helps everyone involved. Think about it.

You are helping your downline by finding new people for them to contact. In addition to helping them, it also helps you. Although you only spend $100 for your portion of a $1,000 of leads, when you think about it, every lead in the entire batch goes toward building your personal business. Wow!

#2 Internet Ads

When I realized that the internet is basically a big electronic magazine, I immediately knew it would be an incredible place for generating leads. We will discuss using FREE social networking websites like **MySpace** and **Facebook** to generate free leads, but I want you to know that 80% of your leads will come from paid advertising in the form of small ads on search engines like Google and Yahoo..

It doesn't matter if your actual ads are in newspapers or online. With paid advertising you will get traffic, which is exactly what you need.

The good news is you can now pay to place small, medium, or large size ads on Facebook and MySpace if you are familiar with these websites.

Here's more good news. I have learned over the years that a small inexpensive classified ad in a newspaper or online tends to out perform a larger, more expensive ad if it is done well. By the time you get to the end of this book, you will not only know how to create a small winning ad, you will also discover over 30 websites which will allow you to place your ads on their pages for FREE!

In the past I've seen this information sold for $24.95, but it is all included in this book for FREE. By the end of this book, you will also discover how to have a full page color ad online working for you 24 hours a day for FREE.

If you were to place the same full page ad in a newspaper or magazine it could cost up to $5,000 for a 30-day run. Keep in mind that building your network marketing business all comes down to exposures, which means we will be using the internet to expose your product and business opportunity to the masses. Using the internet, as well as other tricks and strategies you will learn in this book, you will see that finding 20 people a day to introduce to your business opportunity is easy.

#3 Social Websites

I would like to take a moment and discuss the numerous social websites that are currently available. Some examples are Twitter, Facebook, MySpace, and Craigslist, just to name a few. These are great places to gather leads if you simply know how to retrieve them.

Here is a quick and easy example. If you have been on MySpace or Facebook for any amount of time, you have probably noticed that people go there probably 99% of the time to share their personal lives and life experiences.

What most people don't realize is that you can easily set up a free page on any one, or even all of these social websites, and construct your page more along the lines of a home business entrepreneur.

I built 2 websites to promote my book in less than 20 minutes...

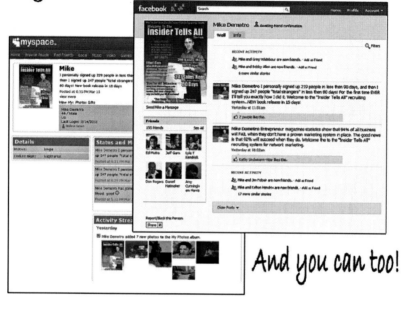

And you can too!

Promoting the book you are now reading

People I added as friends, and YES, they are all networkers

Ads I can post every day on my site for FREE!

If you spend merely 30 minutes a day doing something called 'Friend Request' you can easily have a list of friends in the hundreds, if not thousands, 30 days later. You even get to pick people that are already involved in networker marketing, WOW!

Now you can send e-mails and create postings on their walls with video and audio links all for FREE. This is something you will want to do for 30 minutes a day to seek future business and new distributors. When friend requesting on Facebook you'll want to friend request 15 people at a time 3 to 4 times a day. You'll do this so you don't get flagged from Facebook for spamming. When you run across a Facebook page with a lot of networkers on it, write it down so you can go back and friend request other networkers from that page to help build your list. This is not a fast process, so I highly recommend working your warm market and buying leads from a broker while you're working Facebook in order to get to work immediately.

On the social websites, you will also have other people involved in the network marketing industry looking for you and requesting to be your friend. They will obviously try to solicit you into their home business or network marketing company, and they will be expecting you to do the same. In this case, the person with the best script or the highest proof of income will usually win. Either way, this is a great way to generate free leads and to build a network of people already involved in the home business industry.

The bad news is that it is usually a little harder to recruit a person who is already involved in another network marketing company. The good news is that when you do recruit people using this technique, they already believe in network marketing, so when they join your business they will usually bring a few people in with them immediately. We will talk about generating leads on the internet in more detail in a later chapter. That information alone is worth the price of this book. In that chapter, you will also discover how to use blogs.

#4 Email Advertising

Now I want to talk about email advertising, formerly known as email blasting. This industry has recently become heavily regulated. I do not suggest getting a list of emails and sending out bulk emails on your own. All email addresses which allow messages to solicit business are referred to as "opt in addresses". This simply means that a person has approved or even requested information about home business or network marketing opportunities sometime in the past. The bad news is it could take a long time to build a substantial opt-in email list if you are starting from scratch.

The good news is there are hundreds of companies out there that would love to handle all your email advertising needs for a small fee. You can simply go to Google or Yahoo, as mentioned previously, and type in the search term

bulk email advertising

You will find hundreds of companies offering to send out thousands, if not hundreds of thousands, of emails on your behalf to their readily prepared opt-in list. Once again, when dealing with bulk email advertising, you never really know what you're going to get. However, I believe you will be pleasantly surprised with the pricing of this service. I have seen email advertising specials and promotions offering to send out 300,000 e-mails for as low as $99.

Remember the "break even" rule when it comes to advertising. If you earn $50 for each new person who joins your network marketing business, then you need to sign up two people out of the 300,000 e-mails that were sent out to get $99 back! What if you were to sign up four new people from your $99 advertising campaign, resulting in $200 in network marketing commissions? WOW!

Please keep in mind when advertising through email that the subject line on your email needs to be treated much like a headline or introduction to your ad. The actual body of the email needs to be a short paragraph explaining only, and I mean only, the benefits of your business opportunity.

Follow this with a hyperlink to a landing page or the home page of your replicating website from your network marketing company. We will cover all this in detail in the chapter, "Writing a Winning Ad".

#5 Auto Dialer

This is yet another method you can utilize to gather leads for your network marketing business. At one time or another, we have all been called by an Auto Dialer.

This is the message you hear whenever you pick up the phone and listen to a recording of a person pitching a product or service. Most people have no idea that you can simply go on the internet and Google companies that offer

auto dialer advertising

All you need for a successful Auto Dialer campaign to bring in a fair amount of leads is a good script that is recorded with excitement and a sense of urgency. If you need guidance in creating a winning auto dialer script just go back to the chapter on "Scripts" we just completed. The same rules apply.

When running an Auto Dialer campaign you need to keep the message short, simple, and direct. I like to use a script that creates curiosity, the feeling of loss, and if possible, include a good takeaway. Some examples of phrases that offer good takeaway are: For a limited time only! While supplies last! Only the first 100 will receive this special price!

The company offering the service will usually have a department that will help you with all the particulars. It is their job to help you succeed when running an auto dialer campaign. Think about it. If you don't get a fair amount of leads and create enough sales to break even, they know you won't come back.

Just like cold calling, multiple companies such as tanning salons, pest control, and auto insurance also use auto dialing. A lot of the marketing tips and strategies you are learning right now are used in every area of traditional business to find new business and growth.

#6 Referral Marketing

Referral marketing dates as far back as the beginning of the sale of goods and services and cannot afford to be overlooked in any business. Referral marketing has and will continue to be responsible for building downlines in the hundreds and even thousands all across the country.

The truth is that the referral marketing approach is not fun, easy, or glamorous, but it is very effective.

In view of that, you should use referral marketing in the first 30 days of your business because creating a good income testimonial (30 day story) for yourself is very important.

After 30 days of referral marketing you can stop if you want, but at the very least, do it for your first 30 days. Encourage your downline to read this book immediately, and a certain percentage of them will pick up the torch and run with it to keep your business growing long after you have stopped working.

Remember the slogan we put on our binder: "Whatever It Takes".

Here's how referral marketing works. When you recruit a new person into your business, either from your warm market, leads purchased from a broker, or leads generated from small ads, you will need to ask this question:

"Can you give me 3 or 4 names of people you know who need to make more money from home or can benefit from your network marketing product?"

This is how you can turn one name (lead) into 3 or 4 leads. It is much easier to approach someone with a business opportunity when you have the name of the person who referred her to you. It is a much easier conversation and great door opener.

When using referral marketing, you obviously received the list of names from a person whom you have signed up in your business. The correct and most effective way to work these leads is to offer calling them using a 3-way format. This is very simple.

While you and your new recruit are on the phone, simply click over on your phone to get a new dial tone. Call the new prospect's number and then click back over so you, your new recruit, and your new prospect are all on the phone together. When you have a good script (which we will, because we have already covered that in the chapter,

"Scripts"), referral marketing is very, very effective.

This technique in the network marketing business is known as "Chasing the Business".

Very important: If your new recruit is willing to give you 3 or 4 referrals, but doesn't want to be on the phone when you call them, DO NOT LET THIS STOP YOU!

It is not fun, but is very effective, so pick up the phone and call the referrals yourself and put them through the steps in your binder. Once you sign them up, three things are accomplished.

First and foremost, you have helped your new recruits to begin earning checks by giving them their own recruits.

Second, you have also increased your own personal downline and probably increased your check.

Third, the biggest benefit to this method, besides the fact that you are building your downline, is the momentum it can create.

Think about it for a moment. Let's say you joined a business and in turn, your recruiter helped you sign up some new distributers from referrals you gave him. Then, a week later you received a check in the mail. Are you going to get excited about the business? Sure you are!

As I said before, referral marketing is not fun, but it works. The good news is you only have to use the method, along with warm market leads and leads from a broker for one to two months to get a good income story.

Don't forget, if you have 2, 20, or even 100 people in your current downline who read this book, your job might already be done. That's the power of training and duplication. Make sure to send an email out to your entire downline immediately to let them know they can purchase this book at www.InsiderTellsAll.com.

#7 Streaming Radio

This is a fairly new technology. Once again, simply go to Google or Yahoo and do a search for

streaming radio advertising

What I like best about this form of advertising is that it is fairly priced. I also like the fact that when people are listening to streaming radio over their computers it is obviously very simple for them to go to your network marketing business website or your own personal landing page because they are already online.

You will learn the difference between your network marketing business web page which is supplied by the company and your own personal landing page in a later chapter.

When using streaming radio, you are actually producing a 30-second to 1-minute radio commercial that will play right over the internet. You will be surprised at just how many people listen to streaming radio while at work.

Considering that most people feel as though they are overworked or underpaid, could you think of a better time for them to hear your streaming radio commercial offering a business opportunity and a chance for them to be their own boss?

The last example of generating leads that we will discuss is

#8 Ads in Newspapers and Magazines

This is one of my personal favorites. Did you know that every major newspaper, most magazines, and even TV Guide offer a business opportunity section where people can place a small ad? Keep in mind, TV Guide alone has a viewership of over 25 million people.

When running a small ad you will want to use the same principles of curiosity, fear of loss, and takeaway, but in the form of text.

Your goal when generating leads and using any of the tactics mentioned above is to:

1. *always get a name and phone number, in addition to an email*

2. *break even on your advertising campaign (I feel this is the absolute most important)*

Let me explain in detail. This is where the light bulb should go off and you will truly realize what you have gotten your hands on.

I am going to use small ads in newspapers as an example, but keep in mind that what I am about to say covers every form of advertising mentioned previously.

Let's say you place an ad in a newspaper that costs you $50 and you get 7 to 10 leads (people interested in starting a home-based business). And let's say your network marketing company will then pay you a $50 commission for every new person you sign up.
If you sign-up just one person out of the 7 to 10 leads you received from that small ad, you just broke even. Here is the million dollar question: How much did that ad cost you exactly? It's essentially free!

If you have an ad that is running in newspapers or on the internet and it's breaking even, that's a winning campaign. Keep in mind that you have over 7,000 newspapers in which you can run that small ad. That doesn't even include magazines or tabloids like TV Guide or the Enquirer. This example also applies to all internet ads that you place.

The light bulb over your head should have just exploded!

You see, placing ads that break even is a great way to find new people to talk to on a daily basis without costing you a dime. This is why I said it is very important to break even when paying for advertising.

It's really this simple. When you find an ad that allows you to break even in newspapers or on the internet, you simply put that ad in more newspapers or in more places on the internet. If you are using streaming radio for computers and you have a commercial that is breaking even you simply add more air time to your campaign.

We will cover all ad writing and sales copy in a later chapter. I just wanted to open your eyes to the endless possibilities of lead generating.

When you have new people to talk to every day because you are buying leads from a broker or generating leads on your own, building a downline becomes simple and even easy.

When you learn how to make massive exposures, you also become valuable to the multi-level-marketing industry. You will quickly discover that it is easier to talk to strangers than it is to friends and family about a business opportunity. Like I said before, after your first 40 or 50 calls you will fall into a comfortable rhythm.

The good news is if you are making this many contacts on a daily basis, you are now doing exactly what "people just like you" are doing to generate $20, $30 and even $40,000 a month in the network marketing industry.

Here is something exciting to think about. Now that you understand a little bit more about lead brokers and generating leads, imagine having just five people in your downline who read this book and are now planning to buy leads from a broker and use a good script like the one we have in the chapter "Scripts" to start making exposures like a professional. That's why this book was written…massive duplication.

Let's take this one step further. If five distributors in your business each make 20 calls a day, that's 100 calls a day being made to help build their business and YOURS.

In one month, just a 5-man team would make about 3,000 exposures. That is just like owning your own telemarketing company without having to rent office space or deal with payroll, health insurance, or any of the traditional headaches and problems that accompany owning your own business.

I hope you can see at this point that exposures are what will make or break you in the network marketing industry. More importantly, being able to recruit people personally and training your team/downline to do the same is what potentially can make you rich.

In closing this chapter, I would like to point out that running ads and advertising sounds exciting and is a great way to generate leads, but take my advice.

First compile your warm market list today and start to search for lead brokers to begin the process of purchasing your first batch of leads. Make sure to follow the script in your binder to help ensure you meet your goals.

Working your warm market and leads purchased from a broker is definitely the way you will want to start when exposing your business and product to the masses. This is the cheapest and fastest way to get comfortable with the phone and develop your script while exposing your business to the public.

I am only going to say the word "please" one time in this entire book and here it is. Please listen to me when it comes to working your warm market and buying leads from a broker before you start trying to generate leads on your own.

Remember the story about Steve, the young guy I met in the conference room who was calling directly out of a phonebook? He didn't waste time or hesitate.

He got right to work and through the law of averages, was able to put one to two people a day in his network marketing business by simply calling directly out of the **phonebook**.

Do you think with success like that, the thought even entered his mind to stop and take time to build a website or figure out an ad campaign and lead generating system? Absolutely not!

When generating leads through advertising it could take you a few weeks or months before you find an ad campaign that will break even.

Making your warm market list and ordering leads today is your best chance of creating an immediate and substantial income with your network marketing business.

You will see why getting off to a fast start is important when you read this next chapter, "Writing a Winning Ad".

Writing a Winning Ad

Bottom line: Writing a winning ad could make you rich.

Insider Tells All Notes

Before we get into Ad Writing, let's take a moment to recap on just a few more of the many places there are to place your winning ad (remember a winning ad is one that breaks even).

✓ social websites
✓ home business discussion forums
✓ small ads in newspapers
✓ internet ads and banner ads
✓ small ads in magazines and tabloids
✓ email advertising
✓ post card advertising
✓ Google Adwords

I also want to provide you with a few online locations to place a winning ad. Some actual companies and website addresses here will help you place multiple off-line ads in newspapers and online ads with a simple click of the button. The internet links below will allow you to take your winning ad and place it in 20, 30, or even 100 newspapers at one time with a simple click of your mouse.

www.google.com/adwords/printads/
www.classifiedadplacement.com
www.advertisingresults.com/index.php
www.nationwideclassifieds.com/nation2
www.thegreensheet.com/displayadvertising
www.vizads.com
www.1stopclassifieds.net
www.newspaper-classifieds.com
www.nationwideadvertising.com

No matter which of the forms of advertising mentioned above you choose to utilize, what will determine if you have an ad campaign that will lose money, make money, or break even all comes down to your ability to write a good ad.

Remember, our goal when spending money on advertising is to collect a name, phone number, and an e-mail address, if possible. That is what I consider a lead. Just as important, is to have an ad campaign that breaks even. There will be more on that in a second.

When you start to advertise, you will quickly realize that advertising is a very competitive business. Think about it. Whether your ad is in a newspaper, the internet, on television, or on the radio, at all times your ad is surrounded by other ads - and in some cases, your direct competition. Your first goal when creating an ad is to create a headline that will grab the readers' attention, pull them right in, and focus only on your ad while ignoring all other ads.

An effective headline entices people to take action. This usually means to call a phone number shown in your ad or to go to your website. In the case of an internet ad, there will be an actual link that will appear in your ad that will take the reader away from the page that is showing your ad and your competitions' ads. It will bring the reader to a landing page, blog, or your network marketing web page which focuses solely on your product and business opportunity. We are going to cover ad writing in this chapter. First, I want to discuss the benefits of placing ads and generating leads through advertising.

When a person responds to your ad and leaves her contact information, that is absolutely the freshest lead that can possibly be created. This is the main reason you will want to generate leads on your own. The reason this is so important is simple. When a person leaves her information with you on a voice mail or web page, this is the absolute right time to approach her with your business opportunity.

The fact that she contacted you and responded to your ad means that this is the right time in her life to be presented with a business opportunity. There are hundreds of reasons that a person will wake up one day and decide to start a home-based business. Once you have found a person who is ready to take action, your job is fairly simple.

You will simply need to prove to her that there is a real need for the product or service your network marketing company is offering.

You will then need to prove that you also have a simple system in place that is time-tested and proven that she can use to build her new home-based business.

All of this might sound like a lot, but remember we have all the tools in our binder to help us take each prospect through the marketing steps (video, testimonial lines, live conference calls, or webinars). This is referred to as stair-step marketing.

To see a good example of step-by-step marketing creating sales, you need to look no further than any one of the hundreds of infomercials that play on late night television.

I am very familiar with infomercials and how they work, having been featured in one. The infomercial I appeared on was seen by millions of people all across the United States.

Actual clips from TV and the infomercial

When I saw the system "behind the scenes" and realized exactly how an infomercial worked from start to finish, I was absolutely amazed.

You will see why I say that in a second. You will also see why it is so important to have a step by step process like we have in our binder. And finally, you will see why it is very important for your advertising campaign to break even. Let me explain how the whole infomercial thing works. If you can imagine, I showed up on the set one morning in Houston, Texas.

The set just happened to be a 15,000 square foot home, complete with a red Ferrari Testarosa parked out front.

At this time I was only 24 or 25 years old, and if you recall in my story at the beginning of the book, this is the time that my recruiting and sales had started to take off.

I was more than happy to appear in this infomercial at no cost to the producer or director. Although I wasn't getting paid, I knew that by simply appearing in the infomercial it would help in my own advertising campaigns I currently had running.

At this point, I felt like I had learned so much after teaming up with the direct marketing millionaire who had seen my TV commercial 6 months earlier. During this infomercial shoot, I was about to receive even more information that would prove invaluable.

In the infomercial, I was being interviewed by a gentleman who had appeared in a handful of movies and a few other infomercials. While filming, I started to ask questions in between takes.

Actual clip of us talking in between takes.

My first question was, "How much does it cost to actually shoot an infomercial?" Second, "What does it cost to run a 30-minute infomercial on late-night television?" Finally, my last question was, "If this 'How-To Money-Making Program' we are selling includes 5 DVDs, 4 manuals, 3 audiotapes and a free website with hosting all for $29.95, where's the profit? That has to be $30 dollars worth of stuff, just in materials".

The gentleman explained to me that the person behind this infomercial (my friend) was just hoping to break even on every money making kit he sold. I was dumbfounded.

Why would anyone go through the trouble of hiring make-up artists, set design, camera men, and even a local movie star only to break even? It didn't make any sense to me. A few months later, after the infomercial appeared on television a few hundred times, I started to figure out what was going on. If you remember my story, I had the privilege of working side- by-side with one of the leading direct marketers in the entire U.S. He was also the owner of that telemarketing room that had over 100 employees.

He was also the producer of this infomercial. He was a hard person to talk to even though I considered him a friend. He wouldn't give information freely, but if you figured it out on your own and asked him about it, he would confirm whether you were right or wrong.

What I basically realized, was the infomercial just needed to break even for this gentleman to make a profit. Here is how it worked: The infomercial would appear on television selling a 'How-To Money-Making Program' on the internet.

This kit would contain several DVDs, audiotapes, and manuals. This particular kit even came with your own website. It was really a great deal for $29.95.

After the airtime to put the infomercial on television and all of the DVDs, audiotapes, and manuals were produced and shipped, the owner of the infomercial would just about break even on each $29.95 order. In some cases, he would even lose money on an order.

The kit was worth every penny of $29.95 and would give a person 80% to 90% of the information needed to get his new internet business up and running. It basically had everything needed to have a successful home-based business, except a product that would appeal to the masses.

Following the sale of each kit, the owner of the infomercial would have his sales people (telemarketers) contact each person who purchased the "How-To Money-Making Program" for $29.95, and let them know he had a perfect product they could use with their new internet business.

The start-up cost to become a distributor of his product was anywhere between $1,000 to as much as $5,000. I personally watched telemarketers close two to three sales a day. Multiply that by 20 to 30 telemarketers and you get the big picture. I saw this telemarketing room pull in $150,000 in a single day. The infomercial was just a way to get high quality leads so the telemarketers would have new people to present their product to every day.

Remember, it all comes down to:
Exposures, Exposures, Exposures.

The point I want you to get from the infomercial story is that, when advertising and writing ads, you will have ONE GOAL. That goal is to get a person to take the first step in a 3 or 4 step process.

You needed to understand this before we start working on our ad writing. Think about it. How are you supposed to write a good ad if you're not sure what the ad is supposed to accomplish? One other thing that you should have learned by this short story is the importance of having an advertising campaign that breaks even. Having an advertising campaign that breaks even can MAKE YOU RICH!

The man in the story who created the infomercial went to the trouble of writing a script, shooting the infomercial, and designing a kit that included DVDs and audiotapes, all just to break even. He broke even when people ordered his $29.95 money making kit, but he made BIG MONEY when people purchased his product for $1,000 to $5,000.

134

I want you to notice that in the infomercial he did not talk about a product, he talked about a money-making program. The product came later.

We already covered this earlier in the book, but it's so important it needs to be said again. When advertising, always lead with the money, then follow with the product.

This is called the up-sale. In translation, when you run ads and generate leads for your network marketing business you want to break even to earn back the money you spent on advertising.

When you place a $50 ad in a newspaper or on the internet your first goal is to make sure that $50 ad brings in $50 in commission from your network marketing company.

The up-sale happens when the new distributor in your network marketing business READS THIS BOOK and starts to recruit new people and move product. I have told you that signing people up in your business can make you some serious money. Training those people to do the same is what can make you RICH!

I have already explained several times in this book that training is a very big part of the "Insider Tells All" system. I have even told you 3 times at this point to put this book down and e-mail or call every person in your downline so they can go to www.InsiderTellsAll.com to get trained right now!

You will be amazed what can happen to your business when you have a handful of distributors who learn about leads and scripts and how to use them to make 20 exposures a day. This is called Duplication! Remember, when your distributors' businesses grow, so does yours and so does your check!

Before we get into the actual ad writing you will need to understand that successful advertising is a step-by-step process. For example, with the short story above regarding the infomercial on TV, you will notice that

Step 1, the infomercial would play.

Step 2, it would create a $29.95 order.

Step 3, the producer of the infomercial would then have his telemarketers contact the people who ordered the $29.95 program for the up-sale of a business opportunity that cost between $1,000 and $5,000.

Your ad campaign, even though much smaller, will run much the same way. Let's look at it like a step-by-step process.

For example,

Step 1, you will place ads on Google Adwords or on the internet and get your prospect to leave his name and number on your e-mail or web page.

Step 2, then you will contact your new prospect (lead) and put him through the marketing tools in your binder. Remember, we covered this in an earlier chapter when you set up your binder.

Step 3, then you will sign him up in the business and get this book in his hands as soon as possible, so he can set up his binder, make his warm market list, order leads, and start making exposures in the next 48 hours.

As you can see, it is a step-by-step process.

The most common mistake I see when people start to market their businesses is they try to accomplish one, two, or even three steps all at one time. Most ads I see in newspapers or on the internet give away too much information.

The people placing the ads talk about the company and product right in the ad. They simply give away too much information about the business or opportunity right up front. Here is why that is bad. How can you create curiosity when you give away your company name and product right in your ad?

Another big mistake I see people make when advertising is they lead with their product information right up front. This mistake can cost you big. Here's why.

Let's say your network marketing company product is a vitamin. You want to do some advertising to find new people for your business and pick up a few customers. You place an ad in a newspaper or on the internet promoting your vitamin. Here's the problem with that, and listen close. This is important.

You have now spent money on an ad in hopes that a health-conscious person will see your ad in a newspaper or online and also just happen to be in the market right then and there to buy some vitamins. The bottom line is that is just too small of a market. The odds are against you. I'm going to make the next statement in bold letters, because it is just that important. This secret alone took me almost 2 years to discover.

When advertising, you always want your ad to appeal to the largest market possible.

How do you do this? Simple: Always lead with the MONEY! Remember, if you put 100 people in a room, 98 of those people worry about money on a daily, if not hourly basis.

If your ad offers the opportunity to make extra money from home and 1,000 people see your ad in the newspaper or online, the statistics show that 980 of them could be in the market to hear what you have to say. That's attacking the masses! Just remember only 2% of Americans are considered wealthy. You can market to the other 98% of them every single time you advertise if you lead with the money.

Let's begin with small ads that you would put in a newspaper or on the internet, and then we will work our way to quarter page ads, and then full page ads.

As you will see by the ads shown on the next page, you can create curiosity with a good headline in a small four-line ad that you would run in newspapers, magazines, Google Adwords or even on the internet.

Remember, when you come up with a winning ad that breaks even, you have over 7,000 newspapers to place that SAME ad in. That doesn't even include Google Adwords, magazines, or the internet.

The moral to the story is simple. One or two winning ads that allow you to break even could MAKE YOU RICH!

Now I will show you some example ads to illustrate some points on good ad writing. I will start with a poorly written ad, and then slowly make it better with simple changes. I feel this will be the best way for you to understand what differentiates an ineffective ad that gives away too much information, from a powerful ad that creates the fear of loss, curiosity, and will get prospects to respond and leave their contact information.

Let's start with small plain text ads. When using plain text ads you need to have a really good headline. The problem with creating a good attention-grabbing headline when using small inexpensive ads is obviously limited space.

Let's see what we can do with a small classified ad that you place in a newspaper or on Google or even the Internet. Remember, we will lead with the money potential to make sure our ad appeals to the masses. Let's start with the headline, "I made $1,000 in 30 days", and try to make simple changes to create a winning ad.

EXAMPLE A: **I made $1,000 in 30 days**
with my home business
24hr msg (444) 555-5555
www.YourWebpage.com

The first thing we will change is the dollar amount for the simple fact that people rarely earn money in nice even numbers. So, we will change the dollar amount to make the ad more believable.

EXAMPLE B: **I made $997.47 in 30 days**
with my home business
24hr msg (444) 555-5555
www.YourWebpage.com

The next thing we will do is make the ad more exciting. What we want to do is package the truth in the most powerful way without embellishing. We will do this by simply breaking down how many actual days out of the entire month that we worked.

Let's say, after careful consideration, we realized that we really only worked 5 days total in that 30-day period because no one will work 24 hours a day or 30 days straight. Let's see how that looks as a headline.

EXAMPLE C: **I made $997.47 in 5 days**
                        with my home business
                        24hr msg (444) 555-5555
                        www.YourWebpage.com

Let's take this one step further, and you should start to see what we are trying to accomplish. Now that we have realized that we only worked a total of 5 days in that entire month, let's figure out how many hours we actually worked.

Let's say, after careful consideration, you have realized that you only worked a total of 9 hours in those 5 days for the simple fact that no one works 24 hours a day. Let's see what that headline looks like.

Example D: **I made $997.47 in 9 hours**
                        with my home business
                        24hr msg (444) 555-5555
                        www.YourWebpage.com

As you can see, with a few simple changes we just took a headline that would not get a second look and turned into a headline that is exciting and believable. It does all of this for the simple fact that the headline we ended up with now presents a business opportunity that is capable of earning $100 an hour versus a $1,000 in 30 days.

Let's change a few things in the body of the ad to see if we can create a little more curiosity and confidence. Let's change, "with my home business" to "Are you skeptical? I'll prove it!"

Example E: **I made $997.47 in 9 hours.**
                     Are you skeptical? I'll prove it!
                     24hr msg (444) 555-5555
                     www.YourWebpage.com

The last change I just made was a simple decision. In example **D** on the previous page, I told them I have a home business. There really is no reason to point that fact out. I replaced that with the question "**Are you skeptical**?" to get the reader's attention. Next, I went as far as being a little cocky by stating "I'll prove it" when they go to my website. This should create curiosity.

Now let's do a quick recap on all the little changes that took place to transform an ad that I feel wouldn't get a second look, into an ad that has the potential to create leads.

Let's start with Example **A** and work our way down. What I did in Example **A** was simply change the $1,000 that I earned to a more believable number. Remember, people very rarely earn income in nice even round numbers.

Then, in Examples **B, C** and **D** I packaged the truth in the most powerful way to really get people's attention. You will notice in Example **C** that instead of claiming that I made $997 in 30 days, after reevaluating my home business, I realized that I really only worked 5 days out of the entire month.

Then you will notice in Example **D** that I took it one step further and broke it down to exactly how many hours total that I actually worked my home business in order to earn that $997. Then in Example **E**, I just injected a slight curiosity. I may have only received $997 in my first 30 days of owning my own network marketing distributorship. However, when I reworded the ad to read that I made $997 in 9 hours, you can easily see that this ad captures the fear of loss, curiosity, and even greed, which is most likely to get someone to take the next step.

That next step is to call the number in the ad or go to your website or blog. Think about it. Who in their right mind wouldn't want to make $997 in 9 hours while working from the comfort of their own home? That's more than a $100 an hour! So, you have just learned the first rule of advertising.

"Always package THE TRUTH in the most powerful way you can when advertising!"

I want to give you another example of a big mistake that people commonly make when advertising. There is no telling how much money and how many leads have been lost because people simply gave away too much information in their ads.

Here is a prime example of an ad that gives away too much information. (I will use a company that I know has been out of business for a decade so I don't hurt anyone's feelings).

This company's name was INNOVA. It sold prepaid phone cards and long distance service. You might laugh when you see the ad below, but I swear this was an actual ad that more than a few people spent their money to place in newspapers.

Example A:　　　**INNOVA is looking for people**
who want to make money
from home selling phone cards.
Call (444) 555-5555 for info

There are several things wrong with the ad shown above. First, network marketing companies are generally very strict about letting distributors advertise using their logos or company name.

Here's what is great about that fact. Most ads that have the company name or logo typically don't do well when it comes to collecting leads. If a person sees your ad, and your ad has the network marketing company name in it, why should she leave her information with you? Remember, when advertising, your first goal is to collect the lead.

She can now go around you and do all the research she wants about your business opportunity by simply going to Google and doing a search on your network marketing company name.

One other thing you need to know when ad writing is, that it is very hard to create curiosity when you tell people about the product up front.

You have to give them a reason to want to call you or go to your web page. Remember the two golden rules when advertising.

First, you get the lead - a person's name and number.

Second, you try to break even when advertising.

Let's use the ad Example A, which gives away too much information, and try to improve it. We will produce an ad with no company name and try to create fear of loss and curiosity.

Let's see what kind of ad we can write for INNOVA, the company that sells long distance and prepaid phone cards.

Example A: **INNOVA is looking for people**
who want to make money
from home selling phone cards.
Call (444) 555-5555 for info

Example B: **Get Paid to pick up the phone.**
The long distance companies
are handing out millions.
24 hr msg (444) 555-5555
www.FreeLong Distance.com

Now be honest. Which ad would you be more likely to call, Ad **A** which gives away too much information, or Ad **B** that creates curiosity and fear of loss? EXACTLY! Ad **B** is an ad I created and ran in one newspaper every weekend.

That ad brought in over 100 leads every single month.

Writing good ad copy is an art, and you will need to be patient when trying to write a winning ad. Remember, a winning ad is one in which you break even.

The good news is, once you get the basic concept of ad writing down, it will get easier and even become fun.

You have to treat your network marketing business like a BUSINESS or else you will go broke and FAST! On the other hand, when it comes to ad writing, you can treat it like a hobby. Make it fun.

Go online or grab a few newspapers each week and look at the business opportunity section to see what ads are running. You can get good ideas from doing this. You can also take bits and pieces from other ads to help create a winning ad of your own.

Here's a quick tip: If you see the same ad running over and over again online or in a newspaper that probably means that ad is making money. Take a little time and go shopping.

Call the number or go to the website on the ad to see exactly what the person is doing and what he is saying. I call this "Going Shopping". We have all heard the old saying give a man a fish and he eats for a day; teach a man to fish and he will eat forever.

What I am trying to do in this chapter is not to write a winning ad for you, but teach you how to write a winning ad for yourself whenever you need one, regardless of what product or business opportunity you are trying to promote.

Now let's get back to ad writing and move to a slightly bigger ad that might include a picture headline.

Once again, I would like to show you what I consider to be a poorly developed ad and then show you a winning ad that actually brought me in hundreds and hundreds of leads.

You will be able to see the difference for yourself.

Example A:

As you can see, Ad **A** is breaking all the rules. It is giving away too much information and is also using clipart instead of a real picture of a real person.

Example B:

As you can see, Ad **B**, a proven ad that I have used for years to bring in hundreds of leads, contains an actual picture of me. You will also notice that I did not mention the network marketing company or product in my ad. Remember, I'm trying to create curiosity, fear of loss, and a sense of urgency.

The general public has been getting smarter and smarter over the years. Your ad needs to show a REAL person who is making REAL money. That is what people are looking for.

A good idea when writing ads is to keep the following words in mind while in its creation stage. Below are actual words or phrases that I have used in some of my winning ad campaigns over the years. As you can see, they all create curiosity, greed and fear of loss:

> ➢ Just discovered
> ➢ Never before available
> ➢ First time in history
> ➢ Don't miss out
> ➢ For a short time only
> ➢ Free gift while supplies last
> ➢ The lucky few who discover this product/business
> ➢ At this time only a small handful of people know this business exists

Quick tip: Keep in mind that all you want a person to do after viewing your ad is take the first step and immediately go to the website or call the phone number shown in your ad so they can leave their contact information.

Studies have shown if a person does not take immediate action, your ad will generally end up in the trash and never be given a second look. Just imagine what it would take FOR YOU to go to the website or call the number IMMEDIATELY after seeing an ad. This will help you stay in the right mind set when ad writing.

Remember, when running an ad campaign, the first step is to always get a person's name and phone number from your website or voicemail. This is called generating a lead. I know I have repeated myself several times when it comes to this point, but it is just that important and brings up a very good point that we need to cover.

It is very important when using PRINT ads in newspapers or magazines to always have two ways for people to get more information.

The reason you will always want to have a website address AND a phone number in your ad is simple. Some people might not have access to a computer, and you don't want to lose them. This rule applies no matter how big or small your ad is.

When you are running ads on the internet, a phone number is not necessary. If they can see your internet ad, they obviously have access to a computer.

In this case, you will have a "Click Here" link to take them to your blog or web page where they can leave their name and phone number.

At this point, I don't want to talk about creating any ads bigger than 3 inches for the simple fact that I don't believe in placing half page and full page ads that could cost you $400 to as much as $10,000 if you put them in magazines and newspapers.

What I am about to tell you is one of the most important things I discovered when trying to crack the code of building a network marketing business and generating leads.

You are about to discover one of the BEST KEPT SECRETS EVER...

Are you ready for me to reveal one of the best advertising secrets that you will ever discover?

Here it is. When I discovered that the internet is basically a big electronic magazine with millions and millions of viewers, the answer was simple.

I would use small $20 to $50 ads and place them in newspapers and on the internet to drive people to my landing page, blog, or web page, which is basically a FREE full page color ad capable of collecting names and phone numbers without costing me a dime. It's like having my own personal assistant who works for me 24 hours a day, seven days a week for free.

You need to understand how big this is! If you were to take that same web page or blog, which is essentially a full page ad, and place it in a magazine or newspaper it could cost you $5,000 to $15,000 for a short 30-day run.

Doesn't it make sense to place a few small $30 ads to drive people to your web page or free blog rather than take a chance on an untested $5,000 ad that may not work? Sure it does.

Here's the icing on the cake. If you pay for an internet connection, chances are you have FREE hosting space just sitting there waiting for you to use it. This is where you will put your free full page internet ad.

You can Google "cheap website design" and build a $200 web page that can collect leads even while you sleep. You now have a FREE full page ad on the internet that works for you 24 hours a day, 7 days a week, 365 days a year, for a one-time cost of $200.

But it gets better. By the time you finish this book you will also discover how it is possible to build your own web page for FREE with a few simple clicks of a button. I know, I know - you're welcome!

In the next few chapters, I will go into web pages in detail and even give you examples of web pages and landing pages that are capable of collecting leads while you sleep.

For now I just want to give you one example shown on the next page of a web page I used that brought in hundreds of leads. I simply had 4 or 5 small ads driving people to it.

You can see that it looks just like a full page ad in a home business magazine, but with one major difference. My full page internet ad / web page shown below comes complete with a built-in receptionist that can take a person's contact information for free.

This is done with a simple form built right into your web page that allows someone to fill in the information and hit "submit".
The information is then emailed right to your email box.

(example on the next page)

The concept here is very simple. If this were your web page you could use small inexpensive ads, and in some cases, FREE internet ads to drive people to your site. When a person ends up on your page he can now view testimonials and clearly see that you have a true marketing system in place, which is what people are really looking for.

148

Remember, if you were to put this web page in a newspaper or magazine it could cost you up to $10,000!

Before we move on, I need to say this so you understand its importance. DO NOT make up income claims, fudge your numbers, or promise that someone will make money on your web page. It is unethical and is downright misrepresentation. When you come up with two or three small ads that you feel might be capable of driving people to your network marketing website or one page website that you built, it's time to start testing. I want to give you a couple of easy but effective ways to test your ad before you start spending money on advertising.

The first way to test what you think may be a few winning ads is to simply open your e-mail address book. The average person has over 100 people in her address book.

This is a good test market. Simply email your ads to your entire address book and ask your contacts which ad they would be most likely to respond to if they were thinking about making extra money from home. Let them know you wanted their opinion before you spent money on advertising.

The good news is people love to be critical and will usually tell you exactly what they think, so this is a great way to test ads. Here's more good news: this is also a good way to approach your warm market.

I have done this exact thing before to test a few ads that I thought might be winners, and ended up recruiting a few people right out of my warm market. Think about it. As soon as curiosity gets the best of people and they ask what you're doing, it's time to put them through the marketing steps in your binder. Think about this. If you never would have tested your ad using your address book, you never would have found out that you have a friend or friends ready to take a closer look at your opportunity.

Remember, if you put 100 people in a room, 98 of them worry about money on a daily, if not hourly basis and that includes the people in your address book.

Another easy and quick way to test your ads for FREE is to use one of the social websites out there like Facebook or MySpace.

I built 2 websites to promote my book in less than 20 minutes...

And you can too!

When using social websites to test your ads all you'll have to do is simply post the ad right on your social websites page or wall.

Think about it, while other people on social websites are posting comments in regard to what they ate for lunch you're actually posting FREE ads that are capable of finding new sales reps for your business.

Once again, you never know who will request information and want to know more about your business. I have one more simple way for you to test your ad, and I think you're really going to like this.

Once again, the information I'm about to give you on the next page is worth the full price of admission. Once you have two or three small ads that you feel could be winners, you need to test them.

Below you will see more than a handful of website addresses that will actually allow you to post ads for FREE. I know, I know...you're welcome.

www.classifiedads.com
www.classified-ads-4-free.net
www.oodle.com
www.beatyourprice.com
www.classifieds.bmi.net
www.infowaft.com
www.ad4free.net
www.classifiedsforfree.com
www.adlandpro.com
www.listpic.oodle.com
www.interking.com
www.ablewise.com
www.tnol.com
www.theadnet.com
www.direct-go.com
www.inetgiant.com
www.craigslist.org
www.usfreeads.com
www.highlandclassifieds.com
www.classifieds.myspace.com
www.becanada.adpost.com
www.freeadvertisingexchange.com
www.adoos.us
www.zamzata.com

If you run an ad a few times and you get a good response, you can seriously start to consider that this may be a winning ad. It is now time to step up to the plate and place a few $50 ads online to see how the masses respond.

I do prefer using the internet and Google Adwords to place ads due to the fact that your ad can be online in minutes, not days like with newspapers.

This is where the advertising portion of Facebook and MySpace is priceless. At this point, you should be getting excited about the endless possibilities of running a successful marketing campaign right from the comfort of your own home.

Think about this scenario. You place a $50 classified ad in a newspaper or on the internet. When it's all said and done, you sign up just one person in your network marketing business and receive a $50 commission check. Your ad just broke even.

Let's look at the bigger picture. If your one small four-line ad in one newspaper or on Google only ran for one day and broke even, you have now determined that you could have the beginning of a winning campaign.

You need to do this a few times to make sure the ad is truly breaking even. Remember this is called testing. Once you have confirmed that you have a winning ad, all you have to do at this point is place that SAME ad in more newspapers or in more places on the internet.

Remember, your network marketing business is most likely nationwide. This is where the light bulb should go off over your head. There are over 7,000 newspapers where you could place your winning ad all over the United States, and we all know the internet is worldwide.

Here is another **Quick Tip**: In addition to placing your ad in multiple newspapers and the internet, you will also want to extend the ad for a longer run in the locations it has already broken even.

Here's why. Let me give you an example. Instead of calling each week and placing the ad, call the advertising sales person who helped you place the ad in the newspaper or on the internet and ask him how much of a price reduction you would receive if you paid for three weeks in advance.

In most cases, this can bring the cost of a $50 ad all the way down to $30. That is almost a 45% savings. Think about this on a bigger scale. If you have this ad running in five newspapers or five places on the internet, you can easily cut your advertising budget by 40% to 50% by just committing to a longer run.

If EACH ad continues to bring one new distributor each week, and your commission check is $50 for each new sign up, your ad cost is now reduced to $25. You are now not only breaking even on your advertising campaign, you are actually making money on the front end sale.

This doesn't include the income you will earn when your new distributors READ THIS BOOK and start to move product and sign up new people on their own.

Do you see how big this is? Do you see why at the beginning of this book I said finding 20 new people a day to talk to about your business is almost a joke?

Now I'm really going to show you the power of network marketing. Think about this. You are running an advertising campaign of ten small ads a week in newspapers all over the country or on the internet at a cost of let's say $500 a week.

You are receiving at least $500 a week in commissions and you are putting 10 new distributors in your network marketing business each week. Can you see how you could easily get your network marketing business to $10,000 a month?

Most people think putting 3 or 4 new people a month in their network marketing business is good, and it is, but putting one or two new people in your business A DAY creates the real potential to create life-changing income.

Remember, the rules are simple. The person who exposes her business to the most people on a daily basis wins. That is exactly why this book was written - to show you how to make the maximum exposures possible in a reasonable amount of time.

Let's take it one step further. This will blow you away. Let's say you currently have just 10 people in your network marketing business. They now understand a little more about advertising to find new people to build their businesses because they too have read this book.

Let's do the math so you can see how big this really is.

If you have 10 people in your downline each placing just two ads a piece, that's 20 small ads placed in newspapers or on the internet EVERY SINGLE WEEK to help build their business along with yours. If each ad only cost $50 that's $1,000 a week advertising budget (or $4,000 a month), and you are not spending a dime. That's when you know you are treating your business like a BUSINESS, not a hobby.

At this point, you should have already gotten everyone in your business to www.InsiderTellsAll.com to order a copy of this book. If you haven't, it's time to ask yourself why you are even reading this book. I know you are in the right frame of mind and you are also the right person to succeed in the network marketing industry. The proof? Simple. You have taken the time to read this far. Now it is time to take action and get your team to the "Insider Tells All" website so they can get trained.

Remember, putting new people in your business can easily earn up to $1,000 to $2,000 a month in income. Training those people to do the same is what can create a $20,000 to $30,000 residual income each month.

Email Marketing

Now I want to take a minute and talk about email marketing. Please do not confuse email marketing with using your email address book to test small ads or to run your follow- up campaign. This is totally different. The reason I'm including email marketing in the chapter "Writing a winning ad" is because when using email marketing to advertise, your email itself is actually an ad.

In an earlier chapter, I told you that you can Google "email marketing" or "email blasting" and once again, have hundreds, if not thousands of companies to pick from. One of the positives about email marketing is that you can literally find a company, pay for an advertising campaign, and be up and running within 24 hours. Another positive is that you have a lot more room for a good headline, text, and a picture if you want to include one.

The reason I want to discuss email marketing in the chapter of ad writing is simple. When sending out emails it is important to keep in mind that your ad is not just contained in the body of the email, but the entire email itself is an ad actually starting with your email address followed by the subject line. Let me give you an example.

Below you will see an email marketing campaign promoting legal services. Remember, when e-mail marketing, your e-mail address itself is part of your ad campaign.

Think about it. If the recipient views your e-mail address and feels it is e-mail spam, he will probably delete it before even opening it. You lose. I want to show you a few options of email addresses below so you can see what I mean.

A. thesmithlawfirm@abc.com
B. injurylawfirm@abc.com
C. johnsmith@abc.com

The examples above are sticking to the basic principles of ad writing that we have covered in this chapter. In this case (**C**.) would be your best choice because people would rather talk to a real person versus a company.

Example (**C**.) also makes your email appear more personal and is more likely to be opened. When marketing with emails, the first goal is to actually get someone to open your email and not disregard it as spam. I want to give you another example of how your e-mail address can perform as a headline or an ad. Let's look at a few email addresses below that offer a network marketing business which specializes in vitamins. Let's see which one you would most likely open up and not delete.

a. wholesalevitamins@abc.com
b. newlifevitamins@abc.com
c. BestSecretEver@abc.com

As you can see with example (**c**.), you can create curiosity with your email address. This little tip, as simple as it may seem, can be the difference between breaking even or losing money on your email advertising campaign.

Let's move on to the subject line of your email. The subject line is actually the headline of your ad. Remember, for the last 100 years or more, newspapers have, and still rely on good headlines to sell their papers. In this example, let's pretend I'm trying to sell a book or "how-to" course for $24.95 on how to use Google AdWords to promote your current business. Remember, our first goal in email marketing is for our email to be opened.

You will see by the four examples below that I am sticking to greed, fear of loss, and curiosity when creating my subject line as, time and again, this formula has proven successful.

Subject: **Google is the Best Way to Build Your Business.**	Subject: **Are Google Employees Spying on You?**
Subject: **Five Reasons to Use Google to Build Your Business.**	Subject: **Don't Spend a Dime with Google Until You Read This.**

I hope you can see that examples (1.), (2.), (3.) and (4.) are all attention-grabbing headlines. You might be a realtor, lawyer, or plumber trying to find more clients. If you want to use Google AdWords to build your business, 9 times out of 10 any of the four subject lines above would grab your attention. I told you that the tips and strategies in this book apply to a traditional business, and I meant it.

There are about 10 to 15 characters of space in the average subject line. In a person's email inbox, that is all that will show. Consequently, if your headline is longer than that, make sure the first 15 characters are strong enough to get a person to open your e-mail, so they can read the entire subject line.

Once we have successfully achieved our goal, having our email opened and read, then the real selling begins. A great phrase to keep in mind when coming up with good content for the body of your email is: "Information tells, but Stories SELL". What do I mean by this? Simple! In Example **A** below, let's use Joe as an example. Let's say Joe is a person who is trying to sell a business opportunity which revolves around vitamins. We are going to construct an email that is **information**-based first, then we will re-write it with more of a story line so you can see the difference.

Example A:

Example of an advertising e-mail:

If you would like to own your own home business and become a distributor of ABC Vitamins please read this entire email. My name is Joe, and I joined a business that has a one-of-a-kind, patent-pending vitamin. I am currently looking to expand my distributorship and looking for a few good sales people in your area. If you would like to learn more, simply click on the link below:

www.YourWebpage.com

157

As you can see, the email advertisement text above is information-based. Information tells and informs, but personal stories sell. Another obvious mistake is that Joe does not include a good attention-grabbing headline. Remember, you only have about five seconds to grab someone's attention before your email ends up in the deleted bin.

Let's try it again in Example **B** shown below with a story-based email, along with a good attention-grabbing headline.

Example B:

Example of an advertising e-mail:

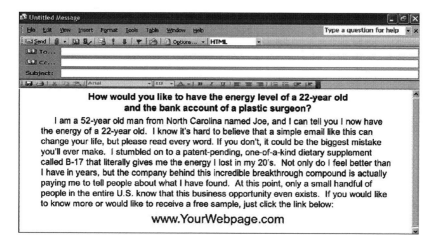

How would you like to have the energy level of a 22-year old and the bank account of a plastic surgeon?

I am a 52-year old man from North Carolina named Joe, and I can tell you I now have the energy of a 22-year old. I know it's hard to believe that a simple email like this can change your life, but please read every word. If you don't, it could be the biggest mistake you'll ever make. I stumbled on to a patent-pending, one-of-a-kind dietary

supplement called B-17 that literally gives
me the energy I lost in my 20's. Not only
do I feel better than I have in years, but
the company behind this incredible
breakthrough compound is actually paying me
to tell people about what I have found. At
this point, only a small handful of people
in the entire U.S. know that this business
opportunity even exists. If you would like
to know more or would like to receive a free
sample, just click the link below:

www.YourWebsite.com

I hope you can see that Example **B** is more along the lines of a story and actually starts to pull you in to Joe's life. People are more likely to read this type of email because they feel it came from a real person who received real results from the product and the business opportunity. This is the perfect example of "Information tells, but Stories SELL".

You will also notice in example **B** we included a short but powerful headline to grab the reader's attention in the first five seconds.

You have ONE GOAL when using e-mail marketing. You want the readers to click the link in your e-mail to take them to your web page or blog so you can collect their contact information.

Remember, the first rule is to always get the lead. By the time you finish this book, I will also show you how to put a blog or simple web page online to help collect leads for free.

Before we go any further, I **do not** want you to feel overwhelmed. This is very important! I don't want you to think you have to start building a website, a big ad campaign, or even a 300,000 piece e-mail campaign before you can start building your network marketing business.

Chances are, you probably have a website through your company that will work just fine. A lot of network marketing companies are getting smarter and creating web pages for their distributors which are capable of collecting leads.

Remember, this book was written in such a way that you can earn as you learn. To get started, all you need is your binder, a script, a warm market list, and a few hundred leads from a broker. With this simple recruiting system, your network marketing website should work just fine.

Also, remember the "Steve story" I told you at the beginning of this book. He was the young 22-year old kid who was calling right out of the phonebook and signing up one to two people a day due to the law of averages. What's the moral to the Steve's story? Simple!

"Whatever It Takes"

You can purchase leads from a broker and even start placing some FREE ads on the internet today. While you are building your business and creating an income, you can start putting the pieces in place a little bit at a time to start building a good lead-capturing website.

Okay, back to ad writing. As you can see in this chapter, we took some weak ads and turned them into strong ads by simply moving words around. It's amazing that all ads use the same 26 letters of the alphabet, but the way you choose to move them around makes all the difference in the world.

What we have just covered in this chapter took me many years and thousands of dollars to discover. Now, you are years ahead of where I was when I first started writing ads and advertising to build my network marketing business.

I hope you can see by now I like to use several different emotions when I'm writing ad copy (greed, fear of loss, and my favorite emotion - curiosity). When advertising, it's really a psychological battle between you and the person viewing your ad. I hope you found this chapter informative. It was written to educate and inspire.

Let's get to the next chapter which explains how to have a FREE full page ad on the internet working for you 24 hours a day, 7 days a week.

Get your FREE website now

You can have your own website online in 15 minutes.

Insider Tells All Notes

Before we get into this chapter, I need to restate the importance of getting started right away with your warm market and a lead broker. While you are taking the time to write a winning ad and build a one-page website, which you will learn about in this chapter, it is important to stay focused and get to work immediately.

This is important for several reasons. I want every person who buys my book to succeed. Becoming a success in the network marketing industry and having a good income testimonial is a big step in the right direction.

When your income increases and your downline grows, it will become easier and easier for you to recruit new people. Remember, this is what we call our 30-day story.

You will want to buy leads and get to work immediately because your success will allow you to write stronger ads and build a web page capable of generating more leads because your income testimonial is bigger and stronger than your competitions'.

So let's do a quick recap before we move onto your free website, or what I like to call your "Free Full Page Ad". You will use small, CHEAP classified and internet ads to drive people to your full-page internet ad, which is really a simple web page that you are about to learn about in this chapter. Your web page will contain a simple form that is capable of collecting people's contact information while you are on vacation or even sleeping.

These are called leads. The determining factor of having a lead capture system which collects no leads versus one that receives a lot of leads all comes down to your ability to write a good ad, which we have already covered. After reading this book, which you have almost completed, you should be years ahead of your competition.

While you are working the business with your binder, leads, scripts, and your network marketing company website that is already in place for you, you can slowly start to put the pieces in place to generate your own leads and have a lead capture system complete with a personalized web page or blog.

Let's get to it!

URL –Web page address

Having a good lead capture system that is included on a web page or blog all starts with your website address or your URL.
If you are not familiar with a website address or URL, it's very simple.

A URL or website address is whatever you type after the "www". This is your address, and there are no two that are exactly the same. A website address is what anyone in the entire world will type in to find you and end up on your personal website.

If you ever plan to have to a lead capture system or a presence on the web of any kind, it all starts with obtaining your own website address. For example, my personal website address where people can purchase this book is

www.InsiderTellsAll.com.

The good news is, a website address only costs $9 a year or less if you commit to a owning your website address for five or more years.

Searching for a good URL is easier than ever. You can search for

Web Hosts

and several companies will come up. There are even a few websites which rate the different hosting companies and give you information about each. This is a good way to do research and find the options which best suit your needs. I chose to use a company called **GoDaddy.com** and have been very happy with the results.

The reason I chose GoDaddy.com over all other companies is simple. They have impeccable customer service. For simplicity's sake, I will be using GoDaddy.com in my examples below to show you how easy it is to find your own URL.

You can simply go to www.GoDaddy.com to search for available URLs. As you can see by the example of the website below, you simply click in the Search box, and type the website address you are interested in to see if it is available.

Start your web address search here

Once you have found a URL that you want to purchase, you can either add it to your shopping cart, or call the live order line.

When searching for an available URL you will want to keep several things in mind. You want to find a URL that is short and easy to remember. Think of it like this. If someone was driving on the highway at 70 miles an hour and saw a billboard with your website address on it, could she remember it if she didn't have a pen to write it down? If the answer is yes, then that is a URL worth buying.

If you are currently in a network marketing company, or about to be in one, then you need to start searching for a URL as soon as possible. Here's why.

I cannot think of a current network marketing company which does not supply its distributors with their own replicated website. Let's use a network marketing company that sells vitamins as an example. Let's say the company's website is

www.BestVitaminsEvermade.com

If the distributor's name is John Smith, his personal website address would look something like this:

www.BestVitaminsEverMade.com/JohnSmith

This is called a replicated site. As a distributor, you are using the company's website address and then adding something after it to personalize it and make it yours. The problem is that any new prospects or customers who are trying to find your website would have to type in the entire website address shown below.

www.BestVitaminsEverMade.com/JohnSmith

As you can see, it's a little long. Let's give it the billboard test. If you flew by a billboard doing 70 and saw the website address above would you remember it? NO!!! I have even seen distributors try to get creative and use something like this:

www.BestVitaminsEverMade.com/IncomeToFreedom

That's all fine and dandy and I'll give that distributor an "A" for effort. But again, the website is way too long. Think about it. If you were on a highway going 70 miles an hour and saw either one of the URLs shown below, would you be able to remember them?

www.BestVitaminsEverMade.com/JohnSmith

www.BestVitaminsEverMade.com/IncomeToFreedom

This is why I say use the billboard test when searching for your own URL. If you think the URL/ website address passes the billboard test, BUY IT!

Let's say that your name is John Smith, and this is the URL to your network marketing website shown below.

www.BestVitaminsEverMade.com/JohnSmith

For a measly $9 you can buy your own SHORT, easy to remember

URL like the one shown below

www.YourWebAddress.com

Do you think this will help people find your website easier AND also allow you to get more traffic when advertising? The answer is YES to both questions.

The only thing you need to do to turn this website fantasy into a reality is find a URL you like at GoDaddy.com and buy it. Then you will ask customer service at GoDaddy.com to point your new URL/ website address to your current network marketing website.

Here's the best part. Pointing your URL only takes a few minutes and is absolutely FREE! From this point on, whenever new people want to go to your website

www.BestVitamiansEverMade.com/JohnSmith

they just have to type in your new, shorter, and easier-to-remember website address shown below.

www.YourwebAddress.com

Get it?

They will end up on the exact same website. It's just a much shorter address that gets them there. In a minute, you will see why that is so important.

Website addresses have become very popular in the last decade. The last time I checked, I heard that 20,000 URLs are being purchased every hour in the United States. Acquiring a good URL that is short and easy to remember is getting more and more difficult with each passing day. People are resorting to buying phrases they feel are easy to remember.

For example, I feel that credit repair is going to be an industry that explodes in the near future because credit score is becoming more and more important when it comes to buying a house or even getting a job. It's no secret that Americans struggle with bad credit. I try to stay ahead of the curve when it comes to the internet, so I bought a few credit repair URLs to play it safe.

The point is, most of the good URLs concerning credit repair are taken. So I purchased the URL

www.CleanYourCreditForFree.com

This URL is not short, but I believe if you saw it on a billboard and you had credit issues you could easily remember it. It even creates a little excitement because of the word FREE.

I also bought the URL

www.OneHourCreditRepair.com

for the simple fact that people like FREE, but they also like FAST. That's where the "One Hour" in OneHourCreditRepair.com comes in. So, keep that in mind when searching for a URL for your business.

When buying a URL think of it as a headline, an ad, or a phrase that is easy to remember. Here is another example. In my part time, I am a real estate investor and a licensed realtor. In the real estate business, marketing and lead generation is very competitive. Everything we have covered so far in this book, such as scripts and writing ads that create excitement, curiosity, and fear of loss, applies to building your network marketing business as it also applies to building a traditional business.

Here's an example. Let's say my competition in real estate in my specific area is a realtor named Stacy Smith. Let's say she purchases the URL

www.StacySmithRealtor.com

Although it is technically a three word URL, which is getting harder and harder to find, it is still not effective because the URL really doesn't say anything or create excitement.

Here's why I say that.

Let's pretend I am a realtor in the same part of town as Stacy and we are competing for the same clients. If I purchase the website address

www.FindForeclosuresFirst.com (which I did)

and Stacy's URL is

www.StacySmithRealtor.com

which website do you think would get more traffic if both are being advertised on billboards around town? Exactly!

I hope you can see what I mean when I say that your website address can literally be a headline or an ad all by itself.

The URL, **www.StacySmithRealtor.com,** does not create excitement or curiosity.

The URL **www.FindForeclosuresFirst.com** works for several reasons.

The average person who is looking for a home gets very excited about the word "foreclosure" for the simple fact that he associates the word foreclosure with getting a good deal. Therefore, we now have EXCITEMENT!

You will then notice I also suggest that he will find a foreclosure before his competition does by using the word "first". We now have URGENCY and FEAR OF LOSS!

Although my URL FindForeclosuresFirst.com is technically a three word URL, it literally creates excitement and urgency. I have actually placed a small ad in the real estate section of the newspaper using just the URL

www.FindForeclosuresFirst.com

and have received calls. My entire ad was just my website address, which meant I only had to pay for an inexpensive, one line ad.

It was cheap, and I would bet my ad got more calls than some of the ads in the same newspaper that cost five times as much.

If you save $30 on one newspaper or online ad because it's only one line, then that's great. Here's the bigger picture. What if you were running ten or twenty ads a week and were saving $30 on each ad? That's SAVINGS of $300 to $600 you just cut from your advertising budget EACH WEEK!

This is why I say that your URL needs to be a headline or literally an ad all by itself.

Once you pick your primary URL/website address and it is pointed at your network marketing website or landing page, it is now time to get to the good stuff and try to grab some free traffic.

I just want you to know that the secret you are about to discover is literally worth 50 times the cost of this book. Why do I say that? The simple technique I'm about to share with you has literally allowed me to purchase a $9 URL and receive $10,000 in commissions in return.

The one thing that determines if a website or web page will make $10, $100, or $1,000 a day, all comes down to one word – TRAFFIC. It doesn't matter how great your web page or website is if no one is stopping by to take a look at your product or service. It's worthless.

I want to share with you right now how to search for and purchase a $9 URL capable of delivering hundreds of visitors a week to your web page, and potentially creating thousands of dollars in sales. I feel the best way that I can do this is by telling you a short story about a URL I bought for nine dollars that turned into $10,000 in commissions.

I was driving along one morning listening to the radio. A 60-second commercial came on talking about real estate. Remember, in my part time I am a real estate investor and licensed realtor. This particular commercial was promoting a service for people interested in selling their homes. At the end of the commercial, it gave out the website address which was

www.QuickCashDeed.com.

When I heard the commercial, I grabbed a pen and wrote down the website address. That day, I spent a few hours in my car running errands, and I heard that commercial two or three more times. I knew the person behind this ad was spending hundreds if not thousands a week on advertising. I knew he was probably sending hundreds of people a day to his website.

As soon as I got home, I checked to see if www.QuickCashDeeds.com was available. To my surprise it was, and I immediately bought it. If the light bulb didn't just go off over your head, let me explain.

His website address is **www.QuickCashDeed.com.**

My new website address is **www.QuickCashDeeds.com.**

Can you spot the difference? I simply added one letter, the "s" to my URL. Let me explain how this works. Let's say the person behind this ad is spending $2,000 a week on advertising and is sending everyone to his website which is **www.QuickCashDeed.com**

I'm simply betting that out of the hundreds of people who will visit that website each day from the radio campaign, a certain amount will make the mistake when typing in the website address and include the letter "s" on the word DEED.

Instead of ending up on his website, they will end up on my real estate website. Can you say FREE TRAFFIC?!?

www.QuickCashDeed(s).com

It's simple. Think of your website or web page as a store at the mall. The reason people pay so much to rent store space inside the mall is because of all the free traffic they get. You know - all the people walking by.

So, along with everything else you have learned so far from this book, you now know to always keep an eye out for high traffic URLs so you can buy the singular or plural version of them.

Whenever you hear a radio commercial or see a TV commercial promoting a website address, always make a mental note to see what variation of that website address you can buy to catch free traffic.

Although people say "all is fair in business and war", I like to think I'm a nice guy, so when I purchase a URL I always contact the company and offer to sell the singular or plural version of the URL to them for a small finder's fee.

Keep in mind that I would much rather keep the URL and the free traffic that comes with it, but I am trying to be nice. You would be surprised how many companies I have contacted don't realize what a big mistake it is not to secure the singular or plural version of their URLs and tell me to keep it. Big mistake. I also realize that if I don't buy them, someone else will because the internet marketers out there are getting smarter with each passing day.

Here is one more example before we move on. Let's say you see a 30-minute late-night infomercial called "How to Beat the Car Dealership When Buying a Car", and it is promoting the URL shown below

www.DontFearTheDealer.com

I would immediately check to see if the following URL was available.

www.DontFearTheDealers.com

That one little letter **"s"** could bring in a bunch of FREE traffic if I purchased this URL and pointed it to my network marketing website. Depending on how much the company is spending on advertising, this could be BIG! It's a safe bet that if you heard the promotion on TV or radio, it is worth the $9 you will spend to get the URL with or without the "s".

The above example is actually a true story. As I was writing this book, I saw the infomercial "Don't Fear The Dealer", and yes, I bought the URL

www.DontFearTheDealers.com

Opportunity is everywhere if you know what you are looking for. Here is why the technique of buying versions of high traffic URLs is so powerful when promoting a home business like network marketing. If 98% of America worries about money on a daily basis, then any traffic is good traffic.

Think about it, anyone who lands on my website from free traffic could end up requesting information and could potentially become a new recruit in my network marketing business.

I also have another option now that I own the URL

www.DontFearTheDealers.com

I can now contact the owners of DontFearTheDealer.com and let them know they are missing out on traffic because they didn't secure the URL shown above and ask if they would like to make an offer.

50% of the time they do, and it's never less than $500 dollars! That's a good return on a $9 investment any way you look at it.

This URL technique also works with words that are commonly misspelled. Here's a quick example. I told you earlier that I own the website address

www.FindForeclosuresFirst .com

If I were to hear a radio or TV commercial promoting the URL www.FindForeclosuresFirst.com, and I didn't own it, I would immediately go and check for the URL

www.FindForecloseresFirst .com

As you can see by the URL above, the word foreclosures is misspelled. I know from experience that the word foreclosure is commonly misspelled.

If I were spending serious money to promote **www.FindForeclosuresFirst.com** on TV and radio and someone purchased the misspelled version of my website address, she would most likely get a lot of free traffic from my advertising dollar.

I would like to point out one other thing. Remember we already learned that when promoting a product or service we always lead with the money.

The reason we do this is because 98% of the U.S. worries about money on a daily basis. This means if we put a hundred people in a room, 98 of them could become customers or distributors for our network marketing business.

Here is why I just took the time to tell you that. If you have a chance to buy a URL from a popular or well known company that is playing TV or radio commercials constantly, you need buy it.

Here is why. Let's say you purchased the misspelled URL of a popular insurance company that is capable of bringing up to a hundred people to your website daily. If 98% of the U.S. worries about money on a daily basis, and they end up on your web page promoting "make money from home", how many do you think will stick around and take a closer look?

Think about this. If a $9 URL only allows you to sign up ONE extra person a month in your network marketing business, that's 12 new distributors in your business over the next 12 months. Is that $9 investment in a URL worth it? Exactly!

At the beginning of this chapter, I told you that what you are about to learn about URLs alone is worth 50 times the price of this book. Here is why I say that. In the last 60 days alone, I purchased my competition's URL for nine dollars which he gladly bought back from me within the same week for $1,000.

I also purchased a $9 URL of a competitor that brought in $10,000 in real estate commission within 12 months, and that is still just the tip of the iceberg when it comes to URLs and what is possible.

Before we get into designing your web page, which is really a free full-page ad, I want to give you one more example in the form of a short story about purchasing website URLs so you can understand how valuable this information I'm sharing with you truly is.

At the beginning of this book in the chapter entitled "If You Only Knew", I talked a little bit about having the privilege of working with a company that had a 30-minute infomercial which was seen by millions of people on TV.

The CEO was a friend of mine and was considered to be one of the top direct marketers in the entire country. In order to protect the identity of the individuals in this story and their privacy, I will simply refer to them as the CEO and Assistant.

I want to tell you what happened to me one afternoon so you can understand why I took such an interest in internet marketing and website addresses. Like I said the CEO I am referring to in this short story was considered to be one of the top direct marketers in the entire country. With that being said, I'm sure you can imagine the schedules, conference calls, and meetings with other top marketers from around the country were a usual occurrence.

One day, about 15 years ago, a small handful of the CEO's employees were privy to a conversation in which valuable information was discussed in regard to a diet pill going to market and how the diet pill company was preparing to launch an estimated 5 million dollar television campaign to sell the pill nationwide.

The company and manufacturer of the diet pill had planned accordingly. They had secured the name, packaging, and artwork. Everything was in place. They had purchased the web address, ensured the spelling was correct, and had a website designed.

By all accounts, they had covered all the bases, or so they thought. At that time, the internet and websites were still a fairly new concept in marketing and sales. It was literally like the "Wild, Wild West" back then.

Within minutes of the meeting's end, the Assistant to the CEO of this multi-million direct marketing company walked down the hallway and purchased a $9 URL that would change his life forever.

The CEO's Assistant who was privileged to sit in on this meeting quickly realized that the gentleman preparing to launch a diet pill and a $5 million dollar TV ad campaign did not secure all the variations of the product name when purchasing the website address. He quickly secured the remaining variation of the website address.

Long story short, when the TV campaign hit the airwaves the CEO's Assistant received free traffic to the amount of hundreds of thousands of dollars in orders. At that time, the CEO's Assistant simply struck a deal with the owners of the diet pill to buy their product wholesale and be allowed to sell it retail, because the company's hands were tied.

To this very day, the Assistant to the CEO who purchased the URL for nine dollars has never worked for a boss again and still owns his own online website that sells hundreds of thousands of dollars of diet pills and supplements each year.

Before we move on to web pages and blogs, I want to say this because it's very important. Although the story I just told you is very exciting (especially if you're an entrepreneur), please take my advice. DO NOT waste a lot of time looking to buy that one magical URL that will set you free. I just wanted to open your eyes to the possibilities, so if an opportunity presents itself you don't miss it.

At this point, you should be focused on training your current downline with the aid of this book and buying leads from a broker to get your network marketing business off the ground.

You should be on the phone within the next 24 hours making exposures. Remember the short story I told you at the beginning of this book about Steve. I went through the time and trouble to shoot a 30-second TV commercial. Meanwhile, Steve was recruiting just as many people on a daily basis by merely calling people
RIGHT OUT OF THE PHONEBOOK!

And, he was getting paid WELL because he didn't spend money on leads from a broker. That is the beauty of this business. When you lead with the "make money" script, 98% of people on the other end of the phone could become future distributors.

After you have made your 20 exposures for the day, then and only then can you start to put the pieces of the puzzle in place to create your own lead capture system. If you work your warm market and leads from a broker with a good script you may never even need to generate your own leads.

Now that we have learned how to create your website address, let's talk about your web page. Remember, your web page is really just a full page ad that sits on the internet 24 hours a day, seven days a week for free.

Let's recap on how the lead capture system works one more time before we get into your actual website. We will use small inexpensive ads in newspapers, magazines, the internet, or any of the other advertising avenues we covered to drive people to our full-page internet ad, which is really a web page.

The small ads that we will place on the internet and in newspapers are designed to do one thing and one thing only. That is to drive people using curiosity, urgency, and fear of loss to our web page.

Once a new prospect has ended up on our web page, it is designed to do one thing only – collect the prospect's name, number and e-mail address.

When building your web page you will want to stay close to the rules that you learned about writing a winning ad. You will still want to create curiosity, urgency, fear of loss, and greed.

I have found that these emotions are very effective when persuading a person to leave his contact information. Having a web page is great because you have a lot more space and pictures to work with to accomplish your goal. In some cases, experienced internet marketers will even include audio and video.

This is why I want you to think of your web page as a full page color ad that is capable of collecting information for you 24 hours a day, seven days a week. If you were to place an ad equivalent to your web page in a magazine or newspaper it would cost you upwards of $10,000 to maybe $15,000.

This is why discovering how to use small ads to drive people to a free full page ad on the internet was one of the best secrets I ever discovered.

When you get some free time, go to Google and search for

home business opportunities

Click on a few links to take a look at some of the web pages that are out there. When you see a small one page website without links, that includes a form to collect contact information, chances are this is your competition. This will give you a good idea of what is out there and will give you a chance to get some ideas for your own web page.

Here's a little trick I discovered that could save you a lot of money when building a web page. You might even want to write this down or highlight it. When you run across a web page or website that has a picture or image you like, you can try to right click on it and save it to your pictures folder.

I can't begin to tell you how much money I have saved over the years by using this simple technique of grabbing pictures and graphics that I could use on my web pages for FREE.

When you are browsing other people's web pages to get good ideas, don't get caught up in the moment and start requesting a lot of free information. Remember, they are doing the same thing you will be doing in the future - collecting leads.

At this time, let's talk about what it takes to create a web page capable of collecting leads. I would like to show you an actual web page I have used throughout the years to collect leads.

Below is an exact replica of a web page that I used to collect hundreds and hundreds of leads. Let's break it down step by step so you can see exactly what I mean. I believe it will give you a good template to work from when building your web page.

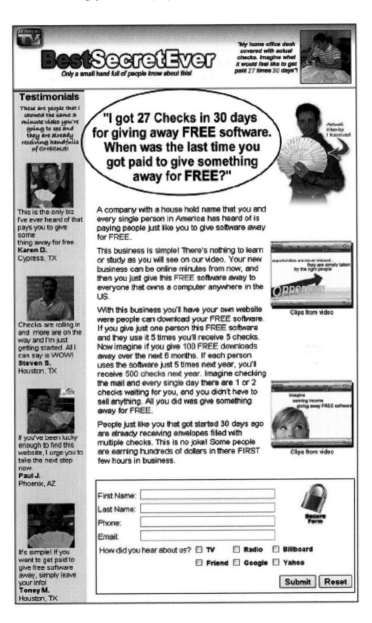

You will notice in the example shown on the previous page, that right at the top of my FREE web page I have a headline that demands your attention. I also include a picture of myself - NOT CLIP ART!

Remember, people are more likely to respond when they see a real person on the web page whom they can speak with on the phone - not ClipArt of a model or a network company without a face.

The reason I have a headline right at the top of my web page is simple. Newspapers have used headlines for over 100 years to sell papers and the formula hasn't changed. Statistics show that you have about four to seven seconds to catch someone's attention.

This is when a person will literally decide to stay on your web page or leave and move on to your competition. We will talk more about headlines later in this chapter.

The first thing you will notice on the example web page (shown on the next page) is that I quickly point out that my team and I are having success with this business opportunity

I accomplished this with four or five short testimonials from successful people in my network marketing business. I feel it's important for me to say this, DO NOT fudge income claims or proof of earnings in anyway. It's unethical, immoral and down right misleading.

I also feel this would be a good time to include the puffery advertising guidelines so that you keep them in mind when writing your headline or ad copy for your next web page or print ad.

(Puff-er-y); Flattering, often exaggerated praise and publicity, especially when used for promotional purposes.

(example of webpage/testimonials on the next page)

After getting the testimonials in place, it's time to insert a little ad copy. Without giving away too much, you want to explain how simple, fast, and easy your business opportunity really is.

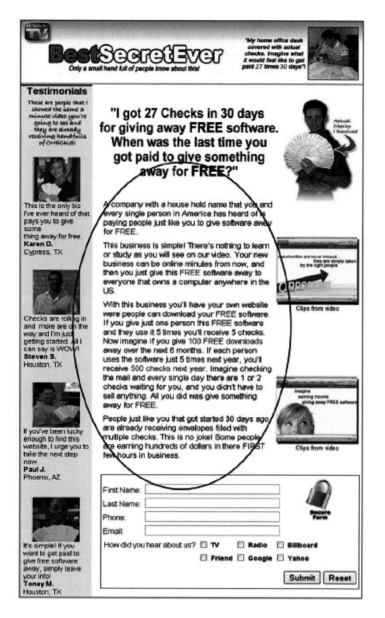

You also want to assure a new person that you have a system in place that is easy to follow and is capable of delivering big results (THIS BOOK). When writing good ad copy, make sure to keep it short, sweet, and to the point. A good technique I use when writing ad copy is to literally sit back and ask myself this question: What would it have to say for me to take action and leave my name and number on a website?

The last thing we will cover on the web page shown below is our order form. This is what will allow a person to leave his name, phone number, and e-mail, which will be forwarded right to your personal e-mail account in seconds. Believe it or not, it's that simple.

Congratulations you have just built a virtual webpage. You will notice that I stuck closely to the rules of writing a successful ad which we covered earlier in this book.

A simple but effective web page or landing page really consists of 4 things:

1. **A good website address / URL**

2. **A good headline**

3. **Four or five good testimonials**

4. **A half page of good ad copy**

5. **Information form**

Your one and only goal when building your web page or landing page is to persuade the prospect to leave his contact information. You will notice that I give my new prospect step by step instructions to follow when leaving his information. It helps to dangle a carrot right in front of him to get him to take immediate action and leave the information. In this case, I chose to use a video. In the ad copy, I also created urgency by suggesting that he will be able to watch this special video that will introduce him to this incredible business when he receives a link in his e-mail box.

This will help assure two things.

First, that he will take immediate action.

Second, he will leave his correct e-mail address.

You will notice that at no time on my one page website do I talk about the network marketing company I'm involved with or the product. This helps to create curiosity and urgency, which are the two emotions most likely to get a person to leave his information.

One other great thing about owning your own web page that doesn't contain your network marketing company name or product is a freedom that allows you to think outside the box.

This technique of using curiosity, urgency, fear of loss, and greed to persuade a person to leave his contact information works in all industries. Here is an example of a website that I have online right now.

The freedom of being a true entrepreneur and never having a boss to answer to has allowed me the free time to also be a real estate investor. I buy and sell properties for a profit like they do on one of the many TV shows that are popular right now. And by the way, it's not as easy as they make it look on TV!

To assist me in this venture, I have a website which looks for home buyers and home sellers. Right on my home page, I dangle a big carrot that offers a host of things once you are inside the website. The only way to take advantage of the services is to leave your name, number, and email to receive your password so you can enter the website.

Example of my real estate website:

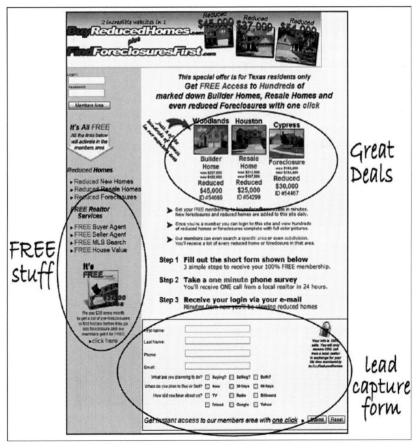

As you can see, this technique of using curiosity, urgency, fear of loss, and even greed to generate leads works in several areas of business. Building a web page like the one shown above can cost you between $200 to as much as $3000 depending on how many links it has.

But here's the good news: the internet is literally flooded with web designers who will work for a fraction of what it would have cost to build a web page just five years ago.

Once again, just simply go to Google and search for

website designers

Building a web page can be done entirely over the phone. There is no reason to meet face-to-face. This will allow you to work with web designers in other states, which I highly recommend.

For safety reasons, I do not recommend meeting people face-to-face or allowing them to come to your home. Once again, building a web page can be done entirely over the phone.

At this point, you now know that we will use small inexpensive ads to drive people to our full-page internet ad which is really a web page. We have just covered in detail what a good web page consists of. You will need the five things shown below.

1) **A website address / URL**

2) **A good attention-grabbing headline**

3) **Four or five testimonials of people in your company**

4) **Ad copy that explains how simple and easy your business is**

5) **A simple form for people to leave their contact information**

Here is the best part. Everything mentioned above that will help you have a successful web page capable of capturing hundreds of leads can all be contained in a FREE BLOG.

Now it is time to deliver on my last promise. At the beginning of the book, I told you that I would show you how to find 20 people a day to introduce to your business - did that!

I also told you that I would give you a handful of locations to place ads on the internet for FREE - did that!

And then I told you that I was even going to show you how to have a full page ad, which is really a web page, online 24 hours a day for FREE, and here it is.

Even if you are unfamiliar with computers, you should have no problems going to any of the hundreds of places online that will allow you to create your own free blog complete with pictures, graphics, and text. Once again, just go to Google and search

Build a Free Blog

You will have hundreds of websites to pick from that will allow you to build a free blog, which is really a web page. This blog / web page will sit on the internet 24 hours a day, 7 days a week, at no cost to you.

Here is what's great about using a blog as your web page. Since you built it yourself with the simple click of a button, you can now go back and edit it any time you like for FREE!

This will allow you to test different headlines and add and delete pictures for FREE!

The only big difference between having a web designer build your page and building a blog yourself is the order form that will allow a person to leave her contact information and hit submit.

Regarding a blog, you will use a simple email link instead of an order form. This email link will act just like a form capable of taking a person's information while you are on vacation or even sleeping.

All you need to do when using an email link as your method of collecting leads is to leave clear instructions right on your blog.

You will position these instructions right above your email link so they will be easily seen.

The instructions can then be followed by simply clicking the email link on your blog.

This will provide you the person's contact information, so you can follow-up about your business opportunity. Like I said, this will act just like an order form and will get the job done for FREE.

I want to give you a quick example (shown below) of a blog that my friend made in less than 15 minutes using **Blogger.com**. He sells a special report online that will show someone how to buy and sell used cars for profit. As you can see from the web page/blog below he has a picture of two cars that he purchased and then sold for a profit.

His blog contains everything a successful web page would need to capture leads, and he built it in less than 15 minutes. The best part is that it is absolutely free.

The only thing you need to do after you have completed your new blog is have your URL provider (GoDaddy.com or whichever company you used to purchase your "easy-to-remember" website address) and have them point it to the blog URL / website address you were given when you built your free blog.

Below is an example of a URL / web address you might be given when you build a free blog.

www.Blogger.com/1001your name

If you have your URL provider point your new web address at the new blog you built, a person who sees one of your ads would only have to type in

www.YourWedAddress.com

Now you have a real blog / web page, with an easy to remember web address, online and ready to collect leads for you for FREE.

Another good thing about using a blog is that it really drives the point home that you are a real person and not a company. Remember, people respond better when they know there is a real person behind the web page.

If you would like to do a little bit more research, just go to Google and search for **home business blogs**

Remember, while you are looking at other people's blogs, you are only there to look. Don't get caught up in the moment. They are lead-collecting just like you will be doing.

I want to give you one more example: a web page that was made by a friend of mine using a website program called **wordpress.org**.

All she did was point and click and in minutes she had a FREE webpage online ready to do business. You're going to love this, she uses her free website to collect insurance leads and then sold them to insurance companies. As you can see her FREE web page even has a built in order form to collect her leads and yes it was all FREE!

I hope you realize that once you understand the marketing systems in this book the opportunities to make money online are endless.

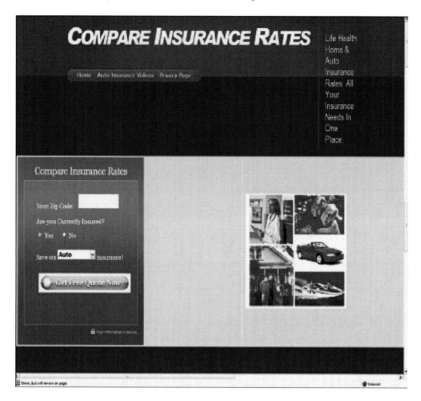

The last thing that she did was point her personal web site address **www. Compare Insurance Rates Today.com** to the new web page she setup thru word press (URL **www. wordpress.org/1476299**).

The last thing I would like to cover is headlines. It doesn't matter if you have an ad, a website, or a blog. A good headline is crucial to your success and that is why we need to spend a few minutes on that.

I would like to take a minute and look at some examples so you can see what a good headline consists of. A headline should grab someone's attention in the first five seconds, so they don't click off your web page and end up on your competitor's.

I will show you three examples of headlines that I took right off the internet from websites that are online right now collecting leads and even sales.

Let's take a moment and read through them and see if you can spot the exact point where they are creating curiosity, fear of loss, and urgency.

Example of Internet headline

"You are just one phone call away from discovering a secret that is allowing people just like you to earn $1,000 or more each week, right from their home computer."

Example of an Internet headline

"Ridiculously easy, recession-proof wealth system revealed in just minutes."

Example of an Internet headline

"Shocking FREE 4 minute video reveals SECRET to at-home profits even with the economy in the tank. You need to see this video right now!"

Example of an Internet headline

"Are you tired of all the hype online? You are about to discover a business that is PROVEN and already has people earning $2,000 to $5000 per week from the comfort of their own homes."

As you can see by the four headlines shown above, these entrepreneurs have figured out that a headline which creates curiosity, fear of loss, and urgency is a marketing technique that absolutely works.

In fact, people outside the home business industry are even starting to use this technique of curiosity and fear of loss to sell products. Here are just a few examples.

The proud owner of the first headline shown below is a dance teacher who enjoyed **$110,120.94** in income generated last year from her website with the following headline right at the top of the home page.

Example of her headline:

"Discover trendsetting new dance moves, enjoy an energizing workout, and get fired up with a dance technique you can't learn anywhere else but here at Toronto's most sensational adult dance studio."

The proud owner of the next headline was from an airbrush artist who enjoyed **$300,000** in sales last year with a website that included the following headline:

Example of his headline:

"Discover the best kept secret all airbrush artists have been using to paint killer graphics and motorcycle graphics, including the hottest flames ever!"

I believe the next headline truly shows the power of creating a headline that creates curiosity, fear of loss, and once again, urgency.

Example of that headline:

"You are about to discover a little-known and controversial truth about the goose down bedding industry directly from an industry insider, so you can finally make a totally informed decision!"

The owner of the headline shown above has been collecting leads which has resulted into **$10,000** a month in sales of goose down comforters. I couldn't make this stuff up if I tried.

This should be a perfect example of how a good headline can create sales no matter what industry you are in.

When trying to write a winning headline for your web page, refer back to the chapter in this book, "Writing a Winning Ad".

Quick Tip: When writing a winning headline there is a little technique that I refer to as "blend baby blend".

What I mean by this is simply, take your time and search on Google for home business opportunity web pages, when you see headlines you like or feel create curiosity, fear of loss, and urgency, print them out and put them in a folder.

When you have collected 15 to 20 headlines you will start to see what differentiates a good headline from a great headline.

You will also be able to mix and match ideas and concepts from each headline to create a winning headline of your own. The "blend baby blend" technique also works when writing a winning ad.

YOU DID IT! You have just discovered a way to expose your network marketing business to no less than 20 people a day and you have also discovered an effective way to have an online presence and generate leads for free.

You have finished this book and now have a perfect blueprint and step by step instructions in your hands to take your network marketing business to the next level.

At this time, I'd like to thank you for purchasing my book, and I hope it serves you well. I truly feel if you have read this book cover to cover you are now light years ahead of your closest competition.

Believe it or not, taking the small step of reading this book tells a lot about the entrepreneurial spirit you have inside.

Throughout this book I have said that only 2% of the U.S. is considered wealthy and 98% worry about money on a daily basis.

I find it very ironic that when you present someone with a home business opportunity you can expect only one out of every ten people you approach to say yes to your opportunity. In my mind, this simply means that the 2% of the U.S. who is considered wealthy are simply willing to do what the other 98% of America are not.

So, once again, the simple fact that you have read this book cover to cover leads me to believe that you are a part of the 2%.

Remember, in this entire book I only said please one time, and I am about to say it again. It is very easy to get excited about web pages, blogs, and free ads, but please, PLEASE take my advice and stick to the basics for the next 30 to 60 days.

Get your binder out, make a warm market list, and go online and buy a couple hundred leads from a lead broker and get to work. As you are building your downline and income, you can slowly start to put the pieces in place to have your own lead capture system complete with a website.

Remember, your goal of 20 exposures a day for the next 30 to 60 days or 30 new distributors in your business, whichever comes first, is the first hurdle you need to clear.

Now that you have completed the book you only have the Special BONUS Report to go, so don't stop now. It should only take you about 15 minutes to read and it contains valuable information that can aid in your success, not to mention there is a message at the very end of the report that I feel could be the most valuable information in this entire book. KEEP READING!

Special BONUS Chapter

What can Google do for you

Millions of people are searching for a home business on Google.

Insider Tells All Notes

Before we get into Google and what it can do for your business, I want to review what we have learned so far. I want you to have the "Insider Tells All" system fresh in your memory so you can get a clear picture of exactly how to use Google to collect leads and find new distributors for your network marketing business. If you have read this book in its entirety without skipping ahead, you now know that building a network marketing business all comes down to EXPOSURES. In the chapter, "Generating Leads", you learned that through lead brokers and advertising, you have an endless supply of people to contact about your business.

After reading the chapter, "Scripts", you now know what to say and what not to say to a prospect, and that a good script has a goal to be met to create the sale. You also learned that you should make at least 20 exposures a day, and you can keep track of them with the aid of your binder that we made. (By the way, you might want to write these steps down on the note page to the left so you have a clear and simple blueprint to follow). Then we covered ad-writing, so you are not throwing away money on poorly written ads that get little to no response.

Next we got into the good stuff, and I revealed a secret that I have been guarding for almost 15 years. That secret is that I use small inexpensive internet ads to drive people to my ONE PAGE website which is really more like a full page color ad, capable of actually collecting a person's contact information. More importantly, you don't have to pay for this service once your web page is in place.

The icing on the cake (up until this point) was in the chapter, "Get Your Free Website Now" where I showed you how it is possible to have a web page online in minutes for FREE. A free website that includes hosting and a web page that you can edit at any time. WOW!!! When I look back on this quick recap of everything we have covered, it looks like the person holding this book has gotten a good deal of information for a great price. Guess what – it's about to get even better!

Now I want to go back and focus on the fact that we will use small inexpensive ads to drive people to our website that is capable of collecting prospects' contact information. Let's presume that you have a few small ads that you created using the principles we discussed in the chapter, "Writing a Winning Ad".

Let's also assume that you have a simple, but effective web page online with an order page like the one we talked about in the chapter, "Get Your Free Website Now". How can you use your small ads and web page to get leads today - possibly in hours or even minutes? That all comes down to three simple words: Google Ad Words. You are going to love this and will clearly see why Google is a multi-billion-dollar company, and in my opinion, worth every dime.

I want to show you right now how to use your small ads and website, combined with Google to have a never-ending supply of people to contact about your business. Did you know that a few small ads and a simple web page that can collect a person's information, combined with Google has the potential to drive thousands of people from all over the US right to your web page, which can then turn into leads, which could then possibly turn into new distributors in your network marketing business?

I am about to introduce you to "cutting-edge" technology - a marketing technology that allows you to collapse time frames and work smarter, not harder with the power of the internet and Google. Here's what is great about the technology that I am about to introduce you to: it's simple - really simple.

To take advantage of what I am about to share with you does not involve writing code or computer programming, or any of the other things I myself still do not know how to do, and to be honest, have no intention of learning. This is a fast, simple, and effective way to build a downline in weeks, that 10 years ago would have taken months, and in most cases, even years.

So let's get to it.

What I am about to show you is the key ingredient in marketing and what I like to call, "Attacking the masses". Here is a visual I want you to get in your head so you can really see how big this is. Imagine for a moment that you are sitting in a baby pool right now - one of those little plastic pools that you can buy for $9. It's comfortable, but there is only so much you can do in it. Now imagine leaving the boundaries of the baby pool, and visualize yourself jumping into the ocean. Suddenly, you have no boundaries. The possibilities are endless. That is what we are about to do from a marketing aspect.

With the power of the internet and Google, you are about to go from the limited, and I mean LIMITED amount of people in your warm market (basically 2 to 4 people a day who you can interact with and introduce to your home business opportunity) to literally being able to interact with MILLIONS and MILLIONS of people. What's incredible is that they are all at your fingertips and are even willing to hear what you have to say, as long as you know how to get them to click on your ad and visit your web page.

Here's how it works:

Did you know that Google actually allows people just like you and me to advertise on their website? The incredible part is that you only pay Google if someone clicks on your ad and goes to your personal website! We will cover that in more detail later in this chapter.

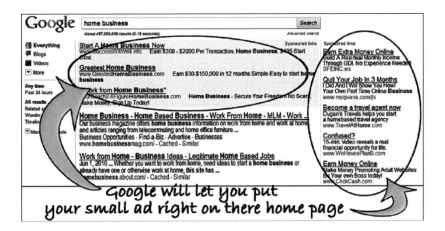

I still get excited when I think of all the possibilities to build and explode a downline with today's technology that was simply not available a few short years ago.

Currently, in traditional network marketing, you are taught to contact 3 or 4 people a day. I am here to tell you with today's technology, not to mention the competition talking to just 3 or 4 people a day is simply not enough.

Not to mention most people in network marketing don't like to talk to friends and family about business so the end result is they really only talk to 3 or 4 people a week if that. That is the main reason why some businesses build so slowly. The end result is frustration and people dropping out because they are not making enough money to keep their interest.

So, what if we could use the internet and technology to find hundreds, if not thousands, of people a week or even a day to share our business opportunity with? WE CAN, and here is how it works. Do you have any idea how many people search for "Home Business", or "Network Marketing", or even "MLM" on Google on a daily basis? Are you ready for this?

Millions and millions of people search on Google on a monthly basis wanting to start a home business. How many of them do you want to talk to? Remember, Google has an advertising program called "Google AdWords" that will actually allow you to put your small ad in front of all of those people.

Think about this: we are just talking about Google right now. That is just one search engine. We are not even talking about Yahoo, MSN, and Bing, just to name a few other websites that will allow you to post your small ads. Do you see how big this is?

I will tell you, when I realized for the first time that I could take out a small ad and put it on Google in front of millions of people who want to know more about starting a home business or a network marketing business, I never looked at the internet the same way again.

Let me explain how big this is if the light bulb over your head didn't go off yet. Let's compare Google to a newspaper, and your small Google ad to a classified print ad in the newspaper. Newspapers and small ads is what the heavy-hitters in MLM relied on to build their businesses back in the day. Just a few years ago, it cost $40 to $60 on average to place a print ad in a newspaper, which was only seen by about 20 to 30 thousand people if you were lucky. That ad would only run for 2 to 3 days, and 99% of the people who saw the ad were not even thinking about starting a home business. And, sad to say, if your ad didn't get any response, it didn't matter - the newspaper still kept your money.

Now imagine putting that same classified ad on Google AdWords. Now it could be seen by millions of people, and the only people who will see your ad are people who are interested in starting a home business! That's the way Google works! But wait - it gets better! The only time you ever pay for that ad is when it works and someone clicks on it and views your network marketing web page. I repeat, you only pay Google if your ad works!!!

Like I said, years ago I would spend $50, $75, and even $100 on small ads in the newspaper. If I didn't get any response that was it - no refunds, no discount, not even someone who would call and tell me, "better luck next time". Do you see why Google has revolutionized the way we advertise? YOU ONLY PAY WHEN YOUR AD WORKS!!!

Google AdWords has revolutionized marketing in a way the world has never seen before. The best part is that this is still considered "cutting-edge" to the network marketing industry. Less than 10% of the networkers out there are using Google AdWords to build their downlines. The timing is perfect. You may be thinking, "Mike, I'm pretty savvy. I have known about this marketing technique and Google AdWords for a while and I'm using it right now".

That's great, but I have a very important question for you: Does your downline know about this? Think before you answer. Remember, you are betting with your network marketing check!!! That is why I have told you several times in this book to refer the members of your downline to www.InsiderTellsAll.com as soon as possible so they can get trained and build their businesses AND yours.

So to quickly recap, we use small ads on Google AdWords to drive people to our web page or free blog, which will collect the contact information of new prospects.

Just imagine waking up to 20 to 30 new leads in your email inbox every morning. Think about this: if a person took the time to sit down at his computer and search on Google for a home business, clicked on your ad, and then left his information on your web page, do you think he is serious about starting a home business? Do you think he is the right person to tell about your business? Do you think it's the right time in his life to present him with an opportunity?

The answer is YES to all 3 questions. If you use a script like the one we learned about in the chapter entitled, "Scripts" to present your network marketing opportunity to this person, I think you will be SHOCKED at how easy it is to sign him up compared to signing up your lazy brother-in-law! It sounds like I'm kidding, but really I'm not!

I hope you can see with the example above that we are using technology to do most of the work for us. Even when we have to get on the phone and work a little bit, technology has made that job easier because we are talking to serious people who took the time to find us and are ready to listen to what we have to say.

This is referred to as "inbound calls". Inbound calls were the key that allowed me to recruit 14 people (total strangers) in a single day, and over 240 people in less then 80 days!

If you are a little nervous about the technical side of things, I want to put your mind at ease.

Go to Google when you get a chance and click on "advertising programs". In minutes you will see how simple Google AdWords really is.

You can also use Google to learn more about Google AdWords.

Simply go to Google and search for "FREE Google AdWords tutorial".
It is very important when you see all the links that pop up to make sure
you pick a link (website) that is sponsored by Google, or at least a
reputable source to make sure you are getting accurate information.

FREE Google Adwords tutorial

Now do you see why Google is a multi-billion-dollar company with no
signs of slowing down? I want you to spend at least a couple of hours
watching Google free tutorials before you start an advertising
campaign.

You will quickly realize that Google is the ultimate never-ending
newspaper, and your ad campaign is really going to consist of a small
handful of ads appearing on Google that you can turn on and off like a
light switch. Remember, you only pay when your ad works and a
person clicks on it! It truly is the fairest deal I have ever seen when it
comes to marketing and paying for advertising.

You will quickly notice after you watch a few Google tutorials that your
ad campaign will revolve around the ability to write a good ad. This is
when you will realize the true value of the chapter, "Writing a Winning
Ad", which we covered earlier in this book.

I recommend that you re-read that chapter to make sure you create a
few ads that create curiosity, fear of loss, and urgency.

The next time you go to Google, you will notice that Google ads each consist of a short HEADLINE, a body for the ad, and a website address.

Sponsored Links

You will also notice that the website address is shown in a different color, which means it will get a little more attention than the body and headline portion of the ad.

This is why it is so important to have a website address that passes the "billboard test", which we discussed in an earlier chapter. Your URL needs to be short, easy to remember, and if possible, something that will create a little excitement. There are three things we need to address concerning Google AdWords:

First: Choosing Your Key Words or Search Terms

A good way to look at this is to try to think as if you are a person who is searching for a network marketing business on Google. You are basically trying to come up with search terms that that you feel the largest number of people would search for when looking for a home business opportunity.

The closer you can get to what the majority of people are actually typing in the search bar, the better. There will be a little learning curve here, but just remember to spend at least two hours watching FREE Google tutorials, and that will point you in the right direction.

Second: Your Actual Ad to be Shown on the Google Page

My recommendation here is to make sure to re-read the chapter, "Writing a winning Ad". That chapter will cover everything you need to know when writing your Google ad.

Third: How Much You Are Willing to Pay Each Time Your Ad is Viewed

Remember, the Google AdWords advertising program is without a doubt the fairest game in town. I mentioned before that you only pay Google when a person clicks on your ad, but I need to explain a little more in detail how payment actually works. Let's use the search term "Network Marketing Business" as an example.

Since there will be millions of people from all over the US searching for that exact search term, and there are probably a large group of network marketers from around the US who are also advertising on Google AdWords and using the same search term, Google keeps it as fair as possible by leaving the price you will pay up to you.

Here's how it works. Google allows everyone the opportunity to get their ad on the site. Your "bid", or how much you are willing to pay, determines the location your ad will be placed.

For example, if a person in New York is willing to paying $1.00 every time someone clicks on her ad, and a person in Texas is willing to pay $1.10 every time someone clicks on his ad, most of the time the person with the higher bid will have his ad closer to being on the first page of Google.

Once again, this is why I recommend that you spend at least 2 hours watching FREE Google tutorials. You will know enough at that point to run an effective advertising campaign.

I want to do a brief overview of the "Insider Tells All" system before we end, to ensure you have the steps fresh in your mind. I want to be clear on what you need to do and when you need to do it so you don't waste any time or money.

I know that most people will want to skip ahead in the "Insider Tells All" system and build a webpage or a blog and start placing ads. Trust me! That would be a big mistake.

Building your binder, calling leads and getting comfortable with your script are important steps that you need to complete before you spend time and money on advertising. Not to mention getting a few network marketing checks will only make your ads stronger when you do decide to advertise.

The first step is to read this book, in order, without skipping ahead. Then, you build your binder so you can keep track of multiple people at one time, and know where they are in your three-step marketing tool process at all times.

You will then fill in your warm market list (this is everyone you know who needs to make more money or can benefit from your network marketing product). You should have a list of at least 30 to 40 people at this time.

Then, you will refer to the chapter, "Generating Leads", and buy a few hundred leads online so you will have at least 250 people to talk to over the next few weeks. You then refer to the chapter, "Scripts", so you know what to say, and then you GET TO WORK IMMEDIATELY!!!

While you are working your business and making exposures using your binder and leads, you can then begin to put your web page online like the one I refer to in the chapter, "Get Your FREE Website Now". Once your website is online, you can then start to place small ads on the internet and use Google AdWords to drive people to your new web page.

Remember, every lead you have, whether purchased from a broker or created yourself from ads and Google AdWords, continues to go into your binder to be put through the marketing tools your network marketing company already has in place for you. Believe it or not, you now have a simple, but powerful marketing system at your fingertips, but and this is a BIG BUT!!! I absolutely saved the best for last. I'm now going to reveal a recruiting secret that **99.8%** of all network marketers will never discover, a recruiting secret that will change the way you look at network marketing forever! You'll see why I say that in just a minute, so let's get started… please get to a computer because the video portion of the Insider Tells All system starts right now at:

www.InsidersMLMsecrets.com

In closing, I would like to sincerely thank you for purchasing my book and leave you with a few of my final thoughts. I have no doubt that many of you will read this book and go on to experience financial freedom and the joys that freedom brings. Just remember that only through Jesus will you ever know true internal peace and happiness. Jesus died so that you can live, so live life to its fullest and never forget that God, our creator, and Jesus, our savior made it all possible.